Doctoral Experiences in Finland

Labour, Education & Society

Edited by György Széll,
Heinz Sünker, Anne Inga Hilsen
and Francesco Garibaldo

Volume 33

Jukka M. Krisp / Michael Szurawitzki (Eds.)

Doctoral Experiences in Finland

Bibliographic Information published by the Deutsche Nationalbibliothek
The Deutsche Nationalbibliothek lists this publication in the Deutsche Nationalbibliografie; detailed bibliographic data is available in the internet at http://dnb.d-nb.de.

Library of Congress Cataloging-in-Publication Data

Doctoral experiences in Finland / Jukka M. Krisp, Michael Szurawitzki (Eds.).
   pages cm
Includes bibliographical references.
ISBN 978-3-631-65156-8 — ISBN 978-3-653-04412-6 (ebook)
1. Universities and colleges—Finland—Graduate work.
I. Krisp, Jukka M. II. Szurawitzki, Michael.
LB2371.6.F5D63 2014
378.1'55—dc23
                                                                2014008004

ISSN 1861-647X
ISBN 978-3-631-65156-8 (Print)
E-ISBN 978-3-653-04412-6 (E-Book)
DOI 10.3726/978-3-653-04412-6

© Peter Lang GmbH
International Academic Publishers
Frankfurt am Main 2014
All rights reserved.
PL Academic Research is an Imprint of Peter Lang GmbH.

Peter Lang – Frankfurt am Main · Bern · Bruxelles · New York ·
Oxford · Warszawa · Wien

All parts of this publication are protected by copyright. Any utilisation outside the strict limits of the copyright law, without the permission of the publisher, is forbidden and liable to prosecution. This applies in particular to reproductions, translations, microfilming, and storage and processing in electronic retrieval systems.

This book is part of an editor's series of PL Academic Research and was peer reviewed prior to publication.

www.peterlang.com

Table of Contents

Preface.. 7

The Finnish Licenciate Degree in Germanic Philology........................ 9
Agnieszka Bitner

Karonkka – Seven years in Finland 21
Arzu Çöltekin

The Technical University of Helsinki and its Doctoral Education 33
Jukka M. Krisp

From Finland with Love – Recollections and Reflections of an
Academic Emigrant 45
Andreas McKeough

Ambivalence, Cancer Narratives, and Passion 53
Piret Paal

Catching Rhythms of the Extended University Sphere 63
Tarmo Pikner

A PhD in Geoinformatics... 73
Rangsima Sunila

A Doctorate in Germanic Philology in Finland – Process, Challenges,
Perspectives.. 83
Michael Szurawitzki

A triangular PhD experience – Germany, Canada, Finland 95
Mischa Theis

Notes on Contributors 107

Preface

This book presents experiences by international PhDs who have completed their doctorates at universities in Finland. This essay collection has been contributed to by many researchers active within the research community in Finland. Thus, we are looking upon a wide range of experiences from the early 21st Century. To our understanding, universities, in Finland as well as in general, apply changes of any kind very slowly. Therefore, the PhD researchers' situations in Finland may have changed to some degree up to now. Clearly, however, there is no empirical evidence for this, and the individual situation of some present or future researcher employed in Finland may differ substantially from any of the cases described in this volume.

All contributing researchers have completed their doctoral degrees (in one case the intermediary degree of *licenciate*, which is explained in detail in the relevant essay) within the auspices of the Finnish university system. This was a requirement to be eligible to contribute an essay to this volume. There seem to be many scholars who, for diverse reasons, did not finish their doctoral dissertation within the Finnish system and/or relocated their research environments to a different country. Eventually, it seems to be a matter of circumstances, partly also of luck, pragmatic approach, and cleverness, how to deal with the completion of the PhD thesis in Finland within the individually imposed time and funding frame.

While reading the different essays in this present volume, the question of why researchers would proceed towards doctoral degrees in a Finnish university in the first place might occur to the reader. There is no clear-cut answer to it. It seems, judging on the basis of opinions presented within this book, that the researchers were 'drifting' into Finnish universities. In many cases, this seems not to have been a strategic and swift, thoroughly thought-out career decision. The researchers who have contributed to this book continued successfully within the science community after the completion of their degrees and today are part of the globalization of science. Finland as a point of embarking on an academic career seems to be a rather exotic place in many research fields. This thus brings with it advantages and disadvantages for an international career in research and science. A deeply rooted involvement in the Finnish national research community seemed to be rather difficult for most of the researchers mentioned. That may be the reason why many researchers who have contributed to this book are now working in other countries, including Germany, Switzerland, Estonia and China. We may find an indication that researchers who complete a doctoral degree at a Finnish university may have difficulties to find a continuing career path in Finland.

What about the Finnish universities? This book offers only a mosaic snapshot of the situation in the early years of the 21st Century. Overall, it seems that the tradition of publically funded education and science as a source of knowledge is valued very highly in Finland. This affects the research community and provides doctoral researchers with a framework which is generally as well as in this volume described as positive. As far as the administration in Finnish universities is concerned, there are different experiences. It seems the political, decision-making administration pushed forward the internationalization of the universities. However, on the faculty and departmental level there seems to be a very heterogeneous picture, with some departments following the globalization path, while others seem to be (too) strongly rooted in the national and local environments.

This volume does not serve the purpose of providing a scientific or empirical analysis of the international doctoral research situation in Finland. It should rather endow the reader with a collection of essays from diverse researchers who document some of their differing experiences during the processes of obtaining their PhDs in different fields and universities within Finland. Thus, different insights become visible and part of the discussion on university education in Finland.

We would like to thank academic publishers Peter Lang for including this book into their program and into the series *Labour, Education and Society*. We would especially like to thank editor Ute Winkelkötter for her continuing support within this project.

Jukka M. Krisp   Michael Szurawitzki
Augsburg and Munich, in February 2014

The Finnish Licentiate Degree in Germanic Philology

Agnieszka Bitner

Introduction

The situation of young researchers in Finland can vary strongly and depends on several factors like the research field and the subject of the thesis. Important factors which guarantee success (or failure) are also the university where the research is conducted, the supervisor and his/her standing within the university environment. Finally, the success depends on one's own work, dedication and involvement. In my contribution I will try to show the situation of Finnish researchers and doctoral students of Germanic philology. I will also talk about my personal experiences during my master and licentiate studies in Finland.

At the outset, I would like to explain the term *licentiate* and its meaning in the Finnish and European context to avoid misunderstandings. In Finland (and the Nordic countries), a licentiate thesis is a noncompulsory degree between the MA and the PhD. Licentiate degree holders are officially eligible for independent academic research at Universities (like the right to supervise master's degree theses). It has to be also emphasized that this degree raises one's standing in the Finnish society and is considered a prestigious matter. However, for the continental European (e.g. the German) context, it is generally regarded as less valuable, and often seen as 'only' a master's degree or even a mere bachelor. This is the case since before the Bologna process had started, the term licentiate referred to different degrees in different countries, and partially does so to the present day, which entails confusion. In Catholic and Protestant institutions of higher education (Theological Seminaries or Faculties of Theology), for instance, a licentiate degree can be compared to the Finnish licentiate degree – it is a noncompulsory step between the MA and the PhD. At the same time, it is a minimum qualification for teachers at seminaries. In Belgium, the licentiate was corresponding to the German master, and it was a compulsory requirement for the enrolment to any doctoral program. In Poland, a licentiate degree still refers to a bachelor's degree, which is a prerequisite to pursue a master's degree. For researchers who did their licentiate in Finland this can mean that their research work can be misperceived abroad as 'degree studies' in contrast to postgraduate studies more advanced than the master's, and their scientific performance can be therefore underestimated. 2011, when I was registering as a doctoral student at the University of Mainz, an employee of the Students' Office, who was responsible for the acknowledgement of my Finnish diplomas, gave me a document which stated that my Finnish licentiate corresponded to the German master. Thus my Finnish master corresponded to the German bachelor. Of course, this was a major mistake, but this example illustrates how incomprehensible the notion of a Finnish licentiate degree can be in other European countries.

My Studies and Research Studies in Finland

After graduating in Germanic Philology from the Swedish language Åbo Akademi University in December 2007, I embarked in the spring of 2008 on a further-reaching academic research project with the aim to result in a licentiate thesis. The licentiate degree entails the writing of a thesis of about 100 pages in length (for philological subjects and the Arts) and the completion of research education coursework. The exact number and field of the courses depend on the subject of the thesis: those courses comprising at least 60 ECTS credits should be the preparation for the project and/or help to gain experience in the specific field. At the same time the courses do not have to be completed at the department at which the thesis is written. Academic activities, like articles or lectures, which are linked to the licentiate thesis, can also be acknowledged as part of the research education. The number of credits applies both for students who struggle for licentiate and doctoral degree. Also other compulsory courses are the same for licentiate and doctoral students. Therefore, for students who do firstly a licentiate degree this achievements are acknowledged for their doctoral studies and do not have to be repeated. During my time there were only two courses which were compulsory for all doctoral students at the Faculty of Philosophy of Åbo Akademi University, namely "The Philosophy of the Human Science" and "Thesis Composition". Unfortunately, these courses were seen by many doctoral students as a genuine *waste of time*, since for many of them it was hard to see benefits from these courses for following through with the own project. The licentiate thesis is subsequently assessed by two experts. A thesis written at the German Department of Åbo Akademi University is assessed by at least one external expert (mostly from Germany). There are only two grades of the thesis: *pass* or *very good*. It is not compulsory (in practice even seldom) to publish the thesis, and there is neither a final examination nor a public defense like in case of the doctoral thesis. I submitted my thesis in April 2010 (exactly two years after starting my project), and in November 2010 I got my licentiate diploma.

The German Department of Åbo Akademi University used to willingly accept new doctoral students. During my studies, there were about twelve doctoral students at the German Department. This is quite a lot for such a small institute with only one supervisor (i.e. full professor). It is also quite a lot if you consider the fact that since 2005 only three doctoral students (!) managed to complete their doctoral theses and got their PhDs, and two more have completed their licentiate theses by now (early 2013). I will come back to this *phenomenon* in the further parts of my contribution once again. Most of the doctoral students at the German Department were external one, thus coming to Åbo once or twice a year for presenting their research during doctoral colloquiums. Some of them have two supervisors, one at Åbo and one at another Finnish university or sometimes abroad (Germany or Switzerland for the most part). For those doctoral students it was often the one and only possibility to discuss their research with the supervisor and the other doctoral students. In comparison, internal doctoral students had an opportunity to get feedback from the supervisor almost every time they needed help.

2008, when I started my research, it was very easy for me to get the doctoral position: the supervisor knew me already very well, the faculty administration in terms of enrolment procedures was uncomplicated, and the faculty secretary helpful whilst processing my application. It took me, in comparison, five months to get a doctoral position at Mainz University in 2011, although for my supervisor the case was clear – some employees from the Students' Office had problems in understanding my Finnish diploma. This happened although the diploma comes with an English language supplement, which explains in detail the Finnish educational system and presents the degree in context of the different European tertiary education standards and even converts all grades into the European Credit Transfer and Accumulation System.

Research Situation

The term *research situation* means for me in the context of this contribution 1) the access to crucial and central secondary literature as well as 2) the possibility of finding of a suitable supervisor as well as other researchers, whose feedback can help in the development of the project and, finally, 3) the financial possibilities of carrying out the project. In the following section I will discuss all these problems.

The situation of the doctoral students of Germanic Philology varies strong and depends on the subject of the thesis and on the university they pursue their research at as well. Unfortunately, and this is questionable, very often the situation does not depend on the level of the research itself and the motivation and work of the student, but rather on other factors the doctoral student sometimes cannot influence at all.

I am going to first focus on the access to necessary primary and secondary literature. Finnish university libraries are mostly rather well-stocked when it comes to the areas of linguistics and translation studies. These library collections do, quite naturally, not solely comprise Germanic Studies, but also serve studies in other languages as well. Thus, doctoral students, who do their research in Germanic linguistics or translation can find lots of relevant, also some of the most recent, publications for their projects. More and more books can be read as e-books. Also the borrowing of books from the others Finnish university libraries works mainly well, therefore the visiting of university libraries in Germany is not necessary for most of the doctoral students. However, there are also doctoral students who do their research in (from the Finnish point of view) unique subjects, and they have to handle the necessity of visiting of German university libraries or – for some very special subjects – German archives. Nevertheless, at the time I was working on my licentiate thesis at Åbo Akademi University, it was possible to get financial assistance (from the university or from the department) for such research stays.

The second point I will discuss now is the finding of a proper supervisor. This depends mainly on the subject of the research. Finnish departments of Germanic studies are mostly small (in comparison to German Departments in Germany) and, with the exception of the University of Helsinki and the University of Vaasa, there is only one full professor at each department of German. Moreover, Germanic studies within Finland is orientated mainly towards linguistics and translation studies (two or three decades ago, the situation used to be different and there were also internationally well-known Finnish Germanists, who did research on literature or medieval German studies). Literary studies seem to be unappealing to the Finnish context by now. For the present Finnish doctoral students, this potentially entails very good possibilities of finding a supervisor in the field of linguistics or translation studies. However, as soon as the research focuses on literary studies, or connects linguistics with literary studies, it can be difficult to find a supervisor, who can supervise theses with such broad thematic approaches. Only very few of the Finnish professors of German language have such qualifications and thus are able (and willing) to supervise theses which go (way) beyond linguistics.

The last (and for many readers probably the most interesting) point of the *research situation* I will talk about, financial possibilities, is strongly connected with the situation of Finnish Germanic Philology in general. Since a few years it can be observed that the position of German studies in Finland changes constantly. Unfortunately, these changes are rather negative and it is hard to say now where this situation will lead to. For many decades, Germany used to be an important partner and example for Finland in many different fields (for instance economy, science, or culture). Therefore, the interest for German language and culture was relatively big. Lately, Finland is more and more orientated towards a globalized, almost exclusively English-speaking world. Because of this, less and less pupils choose German as a second foreign language (instead of for example English, Russian or Spanish) at school (the first foreign language is Swedish, for Finnish-speaking students). Also, less and less students choose German as their study subject at the university level. In this situation thus less teachers of German at schools and universities are needed. For this reason universities *produce* a smaller number of degrees in Germanic studies and get less money for this field. For the German departments, this means strong financial cuts, reduction of posts (or that is to say that vacancies will not be filled anymore), smaller expenses for new literature, research stays etc. About this it has to be said that strong financial cuts concern not only Germanic studies but also other subjects of philosophical faculties. Or, in other words, because of economic measures at philosophical faculties all *unprofitable* subjects (and Germanic philology is definitely seen from the economic point of view as unprofitable) have to live with strong financial cuts. As *profitable* are seen those subjects which educate qualified employees for the industry, for instance in the natural or technical sciences. Such institutes and departments get state money, similarly to institutes in the Arts, from the Finnish government. In addition, they get money from the industrial sector and in this way they are able to provide substantial grants for doctoral students. Doctoral students do their research (sometimes) in turn on very particular subjects, which companies wish to get examined. All that influences the financial situation of doctoral students immensely. In general, doctoral students in Germanic studies have mainly three possibilities of financing of their research. I will subsequently elaborate on all these possibilities.

Firstly, it is (still) possible to be employed for a few years as assistant. During that time, the doctoral student works on his or her thesis and has also official duties, like teaching or organizational and administrative tasks at the department. This position can be compared to the German *Wissenschaftlicher Mitarbeiter* at pre-doctoral level. Unfortunately it occurs sometimes that assistants need ten or more years (!) to get their doctoral thesis submitted. In other European countries, it not allowed for an assistant to work on the thesis for such a long time. In Germany, for example, the *Wissenschaftlicher Mitarbeiter* at pre-doctoral level is obliged to finish his doctoral project (including the defence) within a maximum of six years, in Poland within the maximum of eight years. This restriction often motivates doctoral students to work in a disciplined manner to be able to comply with the temporal requirements of their particular university. On the contrary it happens quite often that doctoral students without a compulsory deadline for their projects and thus work on their theses for too long periods of time. Because of that it is almost certain that the results of such theses can be not interesting anymore – from the academic point of view they tend to be outdated. During such a long period of time other academics can publish their research on very similar subjects and thus go beyond what takes too long to be published. In such a case, the results of a *long-term* doctoral project, can, in a worst case scenario, not be relevant anymore. Anyway, only very few doctoral students can get an assistant post. This financial possibility is, after all, rare.

The other financial possibility for doctoral students in Germanic philology was getting a position in a Finnish Graduate School in Language Studies – *Langnet*[1]. However, this was an option only for research projects in linguistics or translation science. It has meanwhile been decided that there will be no further funding for Langnet, which means this source of funding will soon disappear. Research projects on literary studies are not supported by *Langnet* at all, there is a small graduate school of literary studies (unfortunately not including German literature). Submitting of an application was easy and worked online during the time of my research studies. After about two to three months every applicant received a detailed evaluation of his/her application with grades for each part of the application. This was a helpful measure for reworking the application and, possibly, the whole research project. It was also possible to compare anonymized online grades of other applicants (this is no longer common practice). At this point I would like to emphasize that I have never seen a similar transparency in evaluation of applications and the rewarding of applicants in any other Finnish Foundation (the Finnish foundation and granting culture is a very complicated network (see below) that lacks transparency and has led to criminal convictions concerning foundations granting money for political purposes; so far the university sector has not been the focus of criminal investigations). However, this does not mean that I completely agree with the distribution of the grants and that its manner is clear to me. It is for me namely not clear why some subjects or languages within the area of linguistics or translation studies are being supported and others are not. Some doctoral students submit really very good applications for interesting linguistic projects and these applications get bad grades only because they do not fit into the momentary stream of the graduate school.

However, for those whose applications which were evaluated as very good it was possible to get a full-time position for up to four years. During that time the researcher could entirely concentrate on his/her project. Still, it is for me unclear how the development of doctoral students will be checked. Also here it can namely

---

1 For more information on Langnet see http://www.joensuu.fi/fld/langnet/english/ [12.03.2013] and the essay of Michael Szurawitzki in this volume.

occur that a doctoral student gets a long-term position and does not use this time for finishing of his/her project. Personally I know a doctoral student who had a four-year position within *Langnet* and did not manage to finish her thesis during that time (it took her over 10 years – completely financed by grants and doctoral full-time positions – to write a doctoral thesis of 60 (!) pages – furthermore, the *thesis* consists of only four articles. For the humanities this is a very small amount of text; normally you would expect a monograph of some 200 pages). However, for doctoral students of Germanic philology, it was very hard to get a Langnet position. This graduate school financed some 40 doctoral students in total – from nine Finnish universities and from different language areas. As I pointed out, this funding perspective will soon be one from the past and cannot be used any longer.

The last and most common financial possibility for doctoral students of Germanic studies in Finland is getting grants from private and stately research funding organizations. The preparation of an application is almost similar for every foundation and can be mainly submitted online. In Finland there is a great number of such foundations (if you consider the dimension of the country). Those foundations give scholarships for concrete subjects, for instance only for medicine research or only for the Arts, or for some special purposes as some target groups or minorities as well[2]. Åbo Akademi University has its own foundation, which provides research grants for doctoral students from Åbo. The Emil Öhmann Foundation[3], which belongs to the Finnish Academy of Science and Letters, gives grants (one month up to a year) especially for doctoral students of Germanic philology and for scientists from other fields, who do their research on Germany, its politics, history or arts. However, this foundation does not give grants for book publications. The number of grants given by the Emil Öhmann Foundation varies from year to year. Grants are seen by Finnish researchers not only as a financial support but also as an honour. The diplomas, for the Öhmann Foundation's grants, are handed out during a highly official ceremony in the building of the Finnish House of the Estates (Säätytalo)[4]. Finnish cabinet ministers or former Finnish presidents are often guests during those ceremonies. Doctoral students can receive grants for their project from the Emil Öhmann Foundation only once. Grants for preparation of scientific conferences can be given theoretically every year.

---

2 For more information on Finnish foundations see: http://www.saatiopalvelu.fi/en/links-to-finnish-foundations/ [15.04.2013].
3 For further information on Emil Öhmann Foundation see: http://www.acadsci.fi/scholarships.htm [15.04.2013].
4 For more information on the Finnish House of the Estate see: http://vnk.fi/ministerio/toimitilat/saatytalo/fi.jsp [18.04.2013].

Most of the Finnish foundations award one-year-grants. Contrary to the Emil Öhmann Foundation, most of the foundations offer a possibility of applying for further grants also for doctoral students whom they have supported already. In this case it is (theoretically) possible that the whole research project is financially supported by one foundation. Doctoral students of Germanic studies have therefore a possibility of applying for grants from other foundations as well. Some of them for instance use grants for research stays in Germany which are founded by DAAD (German Academic Exchange Service)[5]. The last three months of the research on the doctoral thesis can be founded by money directly provided by the rector of the respective university. In addition every 'Finnish' doctoral student (Finnish citizen or foreigner married to a Finnish citizen) is eligible for 15 months of small financial support (some 298 € by now and up to 201 € rental support) from KELA, the Finnish social security agency[6]. This is in addition to up to 55 months of non-refundable student support.

The amount of grants given by Finnish foundations is in average between 1400–1700 € per month. PhDs can get for their research post-doctoral projects some 100 up to 200 € more per month. Those grants are not to be taxed at all, but since 2009 researchers who receive a scholarship for at least four months in a year have to pay a compulsory pension scheme. The Finnish state guarantees the mandatory social insurance for every legal inhabitant of Finland by the social insurance institution KELA. Doctoral students who finance their research by grants (and this is a very big group of doctoral students) do not have to worry about their health insurance. Unless, pension scheme contributions for this period time are not taken on KELA. It can also happen that someone who has been working during his whole working life for many years as a researcher by founding his projects by grants will get a small pension because all those research years are not calculated towards it. To avoid such situations, the Finnish government decided to establish a compulsory insurance for researchers receiving grants by a pension insurance of the Finnish Forest Research Institute, MELA[7]. Every year MELA informs its clients about the amount of the contributions made. Thus it is easy to follow the development of the amount of the saved pension scheme. Some Finnish foundations (like for instance the Foundation of Åbo Akademi University) used to give their scholarship holders the possibility of paying a non-compulsory pension scheme contribution to a private fixed-income fund already before 2009. This

---

5   For more information on DAAD see: https://www.daad.de/en/ [15.04.2013].
6   For further information on KELA see: http://www.kela.fi/web/en [18.04.2013].
7   For more information on MELA see: http://www.mela.fi/fi/ajankohtaista/melas-web-pages-english [15.04.2013].

applied to a very small percentage of all researchers, and the new law guarantees a pension scheme for every scholarship holder.

As already pointed out, grants are generally not to be taxed in Finland. They are also not counted as an income for the calculation of the daycare fee - this is another *gift* from the Finnish state to its doctoral students. Some parents have their income on form of grants and do not have to pay for daycare at all while other parents with a comparable income (but gained by regular jobs) have to pay the fees. Here it is to be emphasized that fees for Finnish daycare are considerable smaller than for instance in Germany. The maximum daycare fee in Finland is 264 € per month now for whole-day care (6.30 am to 5.00 pm); for parents who receive grants the daycare can be totally fee-free. In addition, with the exception of very few densely populated areas like Helsinki or Espoo, it is easy to get a place for the child in daycare because this service is guaranteed for every family by the Finnish state. Because of that young parents can easily concentrate on their work.

My Personal Experiences

As I already said: Before starting my doctoral research, I finished my MA studies in Germanic philology in Finland. This is why I had gained a decent overview of the situation within Germanic studies in Finland. Moreover, I noticed the accelerating change of Germanic studies away from a stable to an increasingly unstable situation: the financial support of the departments grew more and more uncertain; at the same time the perspectives for securing funding and employment at universities became worse. In spite of this, I did not get distracted and managed to follow through with my research project, bringing it to a successful conclusion.

Although at times during my licentiate project I felt unhappy with both the situations of Germanic studies and doctoral students in Finland, I feel I have to say concerning the circumstances, I have to consider myself most fortunate: My supervisor supported my research project and provided invaluable help with letters of support as part of my funding applications, as well as providing me with a room at the department. This room became especially important in the initial phase of the project, since my newly born daughter could be there with me at all times during my writing process. In addition to this it must be said that the level of tolerance for young parents (at least at my department) was quite high indeed. I was not the only young female licentiate student *and* mother who combined academic work with bringing up young children. The female professor (i.e. the head of department) took the special needs that come with this situation into account and enabled all of these doctoral (and degree) students an ideal research environment by individually taking into consideration what was needed in the respective individual situations. This is a scenario unheard of for many students and researchers in Germany, despite of the manifold efforts undertaken to improve this situation for researchers with kids.

I have to consider myself most fortunate also because of financial support which I received for my project from various institutions, for instance from the Emil Öhmann Foundation, DAAD, Åbo Akademi University's own foundation or further German and Polish foundations. Nevertheless, I would like to emphasize, that those grants were given predominantly for short periods of time (one up to four months); only one grant was given for ten months. That meant for me that I had to invest a lot of time in looking for suitable foundations, preparation and submitting of applications. Doctoral students who receive long-term grants can spend all this time on their academic work.

Following through with my dissertation was made difficult through a (highly) restricted access to relevant literature. Concerning my research topic, the Finnish university libraries held only some of the crucial literature, and most of the relevant holdings were outdated. Timewise, this led to great efforts necessary to secure access to the texts needed. This entailed ordering photocopies from several libraries abroad and making arrangements for research stays at libraries and archives in Germany and Poland, during which I was able to access the documents I had not been able to get my hands on in Finland. On the other hand, I benefitted from being physically situated and present at my department in Finland. I had almost immediate access to my supervisor and could ask her practically any research-related question needed without further delay. Doctoral students working from remote other locations or from abroad could have been slowed down in comparable situations, being forced to wait for their feedback much longer.

My project was - for Finnish German studies - quite unique. My licentiate thesis was on linguistic phenomena in Richard Wagner's operas/music dramas *Das Rheingold* (*The Rhine Gold*) and *Die Walküre* (*The Valkyrie*). *Das Rheingold* and *Die Walküre* are the first two parts of the tetralogy *Der Ring des Nibelungen – The Ring of the Nibelung*. Wagner wrote both text and music of this music drama and finished his over 20 year-long work on it 1874. I conducted a philological analysis of selected text sequences of these music dramas and showed that an interpretation of the *Ring*'s text requires a constant reference not only to the semantics of German language of the 19th century but also to the semantics of older forms of German (for instance of Middle High German). I also analyzed three Polish translations of the *Ring*[8] of those sequences to see

---

8   There exist three Polish translations of the whole *Ring* cycle. Those are from Aleksander Bandrowski (1903–1910), Małgorzata Łukasiewicz (1988–1989) and Paweł Marzec (2004–2006).

whether the Polish translators managed to convey the many different shades of meaning of the *Ring* in their texts.

My licenciate thesis served as a solid foundation eventually to morph into a PhD dissertation. The PhD research was carried out at Johannes-Gutenberg University in Mainz, Germany, situated at the Slavic languages department. Changing majors was possible due to the fact that I had studied it as a minor subject earlier, and also due to the interdisciplinary nature of my topic partly occupied with the analysis of the German language Wagner librettos and their Polish translations. Moreover, I managed to become supervisee of a Mainz-based professor providing the necessary expertise by being among the leading experts in drama translation for the Polish-German language pair.

The research questions raised in my project might seem odd, if not entirely irrelevant in an exclusively Finnish research setting. In a German language sphere, however, regardless of Germanic or Slavic studies (or even theatre, music, culture or political science disciplines) my topic/project with its *Wagner* bias is more or less automatically of high relevance and worth researching. Against this backdrop I have had more possibilities of communicating and interacting with colleagues who are explicitly Wagner scholars than I could have had in Finland. I lacked this opportunity while still based in Finland, which partially slowed down the project's evolvement. In spite of this, I cannot consider writing my licenciate thesis as a waste of time, since my supervisor taught me solid philological approaches I could rely upon whilst completing my PhD.

References

Bitner-Szurawitzki, A. (2010): *"So verfluch'ich die Liebe!" Eine linguistische Analyse des 'literarischen Leitmotivs der Liebe' im Ausgangstext und drei polnischen Übersetzungen von Richard Wagners Musikdrama "Der Ring des Nibelungen" am Beispiel der 'Szene des Raubes des Golds', "Das Rheingold", erster Akt, und der 'Liebesszene zwischen Sieglinde und Siegmund', "Die Walküre", erster Akt*. Licentiate thesis. Åbo Akademi University. Manuscript. 201 leaves.

Bitner-Szurawitzki, A. (2013): *Wagner als Philologe: Textarchäologische Erschließung des* Ring des Nibelungen *und dreier polnischer Übersetzungen*. Würzburg: Königshausen & Neumann. 237 pp.

Bandrowski, A. (1903): *Zygfryd*. L.K. Górski. Kraków.

Bandrowski, A. (1906): *Walkirya*. L.K. Górski. Kraków.

Bandrowski, A. (1908): *Złoto Renu*. W.L. Anczyc i spółka. Kraków.

Bandrowski, A. (1910): *Zmierzch bogów*. W.L. Anczyc i spółka. Kraków.

Łukasiewicz, M. (1988): *Walkiria*. Teatr Wielki. Warszawa.

Łukasiewicz, M. (1988a): *Złoto Renu*. Teatr Wielki. Warszawa.
Łukasiewicz, M. (1989): *Zmierzch bogów*. Teatr Wielki. Warszawa.
Łukasiewicz, M. (1989a): *Zygfryd*. Teatr Wielki. Warszawa.
Marzec, P. (2004): *Złoto Renu*. Manuscript.
Marzec, P. (2004a): *Walkiria*. Manuscript.
Marzec, P. (2005): *Zygfryd*. Manuscript.
Marzec, P. (2006): *Zmierzch bogów*. Manuscript.
Wagner, R. (2009): *Der Ring des Nibelungen*. Philip Reclam. Stuttgart.

Karonkka – Seven years in Finland

Arzu Çöltekin

Prologue – or disclaimer

This text below is a brief 'memoir' I jotted down upon a request by the editors of this book (who are also friends). Thus, it is merely a narrative of my *entirely subjective* experiences, thoughts that crossed my mind and my opinions biased by my own upbringing, exposure to my share of life's random chaos. That is to say, the text below is not a result of exhaustive (or non-exhaustive, to be clear) research, and should be read as such.

I spent roughly seven (consecutive) years in Finland doing a PhD and a short post-doc phase. I enjoyed a lot of this time and have benefitted greatly from being there. However, as one would expect, I also struggled with some aspects of living in a foreign culture, trying to function in a foreign language (in English, and in this configuration, everyone's second language). I apologize in advance for the stereotypes this text might be serving. I have been a subject to gender and nationality stereotyping myself and at times I found it well-intended and humorous, while at times I found it unfair and thus disliked it immensely as some people feel superior based on their group identity (read, gender, race, nationality, profession, family, sports club... you name it) and discriminate against others. I think you will agree that this is not fair, because the individual didn't "earn" a nationality, gender, family or race. This sort of thing is not an achievement (not even a choice) to feel good/clever/bad/not-so-clever about and honestly the concept some call 'birth right' makes me think (why should we have different rights than others because of a cosmic coincidence that we are born to a poorer or richer family, nation or whatever other tribe?). I suppose this makes me a baseline egalitarian. And, I don't mean equal function (i.e. everyone can lift the same amount of weight) but equal rights (i.e. you should be reasonably rewarded for lifting more weight, but you shouldn't have more rights in all areas of life – and most definitely not because your sibling, cousin or your neighbor's great grandfather could lift more weight. Having more rights globally because of nationality, for example, would be because your neighbor's great-great-grandfather may have achieved something (might even be literally so that they could lift more weight).

Anyway, what I am trying to say is that, I wish not to help build more and/or stronger stereotypes and 'prime' the reader to treat people differently before getting to know them as individuals. Thus I hope that the reader (you) will keep in mind how subjective and how conversational the anecdotes below are and would apply only to me and only during this time span I was there, which is already quite a while ago (nearly 7 years ago, I moved to Switzerland).

One afternoon a colleague walks in to my office

After considerable email, fax and snail mail correspondence (yes, it was the time when we still used fax machines) to sort out paper work, I arrived at Helsinki on a beautiful June 2nd; funded by CIMO[1] for a 4-month research stay at Helsinki University of Technology[2] (strange to think it doesn't exist anymore). Up until a few months before that, I didn't know such a thing as CIMO existed at all, neither did I know that it would be my benefactor which provided the 'seed funding' that was about to change my life. And I most definitely didn't plan to go to Finland for a PhD back then. It just wasn't on my "radar".

I was considering foreign universities because once you decide to try science as a profession, international experiences are highly encouraged, besides I was drawn to discover something new at the time (probably that didn't change all that much). I corresponded with some universities in the USA and in Australia since I spoke (some form of) English, but no other foreign language, not enough to study in it anyway. Therefore, I didn't imagine I could function in mainland Europe as I wasn't sure how much 'knowing only English' would help. The UK would've been an option (being *almost* in Europe, that is) but at the time the UK was increasingly getting a bad reputation that they were treating foreign students who come with their own scholarships or money as 'clients' and they didn't care to teach – it was only hearsay via friends, but was discouraging enough. Besides 'it rained all the time'! (Ok, admittedly, if weather had been an argument, I shouldn't have ended up in Finland).

As I was preparing my applications and taking all sorts of tests for this and that skill or ability, people around me learned that I had intentions to go abroad to get a PhD. One of those days, a co-worker at my home university walked in to the thick-stone-walled and thus slightly chilly (note that in an Istanbul summer this is

---

1   Center for International Mobility, Finland, http://www.cimo.fi
2   Helsinki University of Technology, which we fondly called the HUT, was merged with two other universities and has become Aalto University in 2010.

desirable) lab, with a call for applications (for a scholarship) in his hand and said "Arzu, this seems right for you". If I would get the scholarship, I would get to go to Finland for 4–9 months on a research exchange program.

At the time I worked at the Geomatics[3] department, but we were given an office in the Architecture building for our lab space needs and the fact that we offered at least one geoinformatics class to the students of architecture. "My office" then, therefore, was a photogrammetry[4] lab with really fascinating optical machinery (binoculars, pedals and plotters were connected, took some skills to operate) and couple of desks for interns. It was (as mentioned earlier) chilly because it was said to be converted form an old royal stable, and royal horses were, for multiple reasons not clear to me, were placed behind 1m thick walls. University main campus was converted form a palace altogether and had old beautiful buildings (one with towers to host birds, another with frescos to watch on its ceilings), a stunning garden with exotic trees and nice spots to hangout. Kış Bahçesi (winter garden) and Aşıklar Yolu (lovers' path) were two of the very nice ones that comes to mind. You must find your way there if you are ever in Istanbul for a modest, pleasant break. Anyway, it was lovely to walk in to 'my office' in hot summer days.

But I'm digressing. I mean to say that I remember the moment. My co-worker left the call-for-applications leaflet and I stashed it in the drawer of my (somewhat stained) blue-top desk (I think I never have seen a blue-top desk since that one, I wonder why we don't get more colors with working desks). I didn't take a note of the deadline on my agenda, and then moved on to deal with everyday business and Istanbul's vivid social life. If I wasn't asked (by the colleague who brought me the ad) after couple of days, I could've very well missed the deadline. But he did remind me of it (probably my co-workers were all in it, trying to get rid of me), and I applied. Soon after that, I was called for an interview in Ankara[5], probably thanks to a previous IASTE[6] exchange which I have received against many odds and spent a summer in Holland (another story, but when I say against many odds, what I mean to say is that my 'ordinary state high school' education in a suburb of Istanbul didn't really warrant the chances). For the CIMO application I more than

---

3   A technical field often positioned under civil engineering faculty. It mainly consists of producing, processing and visualization of geographic information by means of surveying and (mostly) applied mathematics.
4   A sub-discipline of geographic information related professions where precise maps and three-dimensional (city, terrain or object) models are obtained form photographs as input.
5   Incidentally the word 'ankara' means 'harsh' in the Finnish language. Just so that you know.
6   The International Association for the Exchange of Students for Technical Experience: http://www.iaeste.org/

gladly went to Ankara for an interview, despite the fact that one of my professors said it was a 'waste of time' and it probably was already decided who gets the scholarship (corruption and nepotism unfortunately is not unthinkable in Turkey, to put it mildly). I was a little discouraged, as I had no 'connections', but I did get my traineeships and my previous job in a company and my job at the university without any 'connections', so I still had some faith that it was worth trying if no one supported my application because of personal connections. I wanted to try nonetheless. My brother lived in Ankara back then and I enjoyed visiting him – at worst it would be a fun trip. Well, it turned out the game wasn't fixed. Before I knew it, I was running from office to office sorting (loads of) paperwork to spend my summer in what was known in my household as "Ak Zambaklar Ülkesi" (The Country of White Lilies, a book by Grigory Petrov, which is known to many Turkish teachers as it focuses on education and was once an officially recommended book)[7].

Finland is just wonderful[8]

This was right after I got my MSc degree in Istanbul, when I was young and was fascinated by (Turkish stereotype of) the Northern European countries. According to the legend, the sun did set for six months and people read books all the time (and more than anywhere else) and politics was fair and uncorrupt. It sounded like a wonderful place to get to know. And it turned out to be all true (roughly, at least). The sun indeed did not set that June[9], and people are indeed more literate than average and politics indeed seems to be less corrupted than elsewhere. So I got what I was looking for, and then some more. Of course as you all know, life tends to be more complex than a three-item bulleted list, but I had a pretty good looking list:

- The sun shines 56 days in Helsinki per year (>300 days in Istanbul)
- Finnish kids score much higher than the next best in OECD[10] (Turkey, not so much); referred to as the PISA studies
- Finland scores great in the corruption index (Turkey, not so much)

---

7 http://tr.wikipedia.org/wiki/Beyaz_Zambaklar_%C3%9Clkesinde
8 You *have to* listen to Monty Python's Finland song: http://www.youtube.com/watch?v= 7rwc3VGvlRY, if you're reading this book.
9 It's not six months, if you are wondering, not in Helsinki anyway.
10 http://www.smithsonianmag.com/innovation/why-are-finlands-schools-successful-49859555/

What would these things say about your everyday life and your academic life in Finland? I knew it was going to be colder, but a cool summer was not so bad, everyone were going to be such bookworms and was I looking forward to the intellectual conversations with honest and well-read people. Besides, we were told in school that we were linguistically 'cousins' (somehow they got lost in geography and ended up far north) – so I was under a naïve illusion that maybe learning the language wasn't going to be a big deal and during one summer I could learn a lot. After all, I learned English with all its eccentricity (if your first language is Turkish, English can appear completely counter-intuitive with its syntax and logic). It was looking good!

So I arrived. It was the summer of 1997, I was full of positive thoughts, and had a wonderful summer. My advisor, upon hearing my interest in indoor modeling after my MSc that was on a 'campus information system' but was all in two-dimensions, offered me a modest task of creating an indoor "walk-through" model (like you're walking inside a building) in 3D to put it *online* – mind you, we didn't have WebGL[11] in 1999, VRML[12] was just gaining momentum and it was kind of exciting as it could do multimedia and transparency and photo-realism, *all on the Internet*. If you are a complete non-techie, you can just classify this bit under 'nerd excitement' and keep reading. I started to work through my little project, and discover the work culture slowly, as well as the life outside work.

The life outside work seemed like mainly heavy drinking, and in one occasion climbing the roof of a church to watch sunset and sunrise which are not that far apart in summer nights. While the roof thing did not repeat, the socializing continued to be mainly heavy drinking and sauna parties[13] during my seven years in Finland.[14]

At some point (and let this be that point) I have to note that the country is also very nice for anything outdoors during summer. Ok, the summers are short[15]. But you can kayak in the countless lakes and the Baltic Sea, pick wild raspberries by hand and enjoy hikes in superbly fresh air in the forests that are everywhere and

---

11 http://en.wikipedia.org/wiki/WebGL
12 http://en.wikipedia.org/wiki/VRML
13 You dress up, put on makeup, go to a party. It can be in someone's home. Maybe you take a drink. Then they say 'how about sauna before dinner', and soon everyone is standing in their towels, their hair all messed up, makeup is gone and the cheeks are red. And you are holding a beer in your hand. That's a sauna party. And no, it is almost never 'mixed'.
14 Reference to the mainstream movie called *Seven Years in Tibet*. No "deeper" meaning but a free association based on common words.
15 My favorite Nordic joke is probably this: *"Of course we have summers in Finland. I remember the last one was on a Thursday"*.

plenty. During its summer, Finland is beautiful with plenty of green and blue. It is a bit flat, which can make the scenery a little less majestic than mountains but apparently it helps with biking and walking.

While the wonderful summer presented itself with countless outdoor and indoor social events organized and structured through international student organizations at the university, things were a bit less *structured* at work somehow. I was not asked for a progress report or any regular meetings. In fact it seemed as if everyone showed up as they pleased and nobody was really bossing anybody (perhaps most universities are like this around the world). I had a nice office, it had everything an office needed and a sink with a water tap (I think that's something I've only seen in Finland)– it was in the main building which was convenient for going to lunch or to the two shops, one bank, one post office and one pharmacy that we had on campus. I shared my office with a Greek fellow. Being another foreign student and originating from a neighboring country, his experiences were very helpful in orienting myself in this new environment. As we shared the space, we discovered that we also shared countless words which were borrowed from each other's languages, our cuisine was nearly identical (and if 'you are what you eat'. well, I'll leave the conclusion of this one to you). Anyway, I finished my work and had a really good time that summer.

The summer is over – now on to serious business

Towards the end of the summer, in a conversation with my advisor I told that I would maybe go to the USA for a PhD. I believe it was in that conversation that I was told it would be also possible for me to do my PhD in Finland (they already had couple of others who did their work in English). I thought to myself, why not – closer to 'home' (no time zones to care about, travel time not comparable to US or Oz), a special experience with dark/cold/light –besides the country had a really good reputation in technical fields (motherland of Linux and Nokia) – besides there were other foreign students and English seemed to be no problem. Everyone spoke English and with a fairly sophisticated vocabulary, too, even if with some accent and a bit slower, but that was all good as English was also a second language to me – I had no experience in living in a country long-term without understanding the local language and there was no way I could guess the cost of it at the time. It seemed like because everyone could speak English, including the service people and bus drivers, one could function perfectly. I was also told that if I decide to do my PhD in Finland, I should know that PhD students were more *independent* than in many places, that is, if I chose to go to the USA, someone (e.g. the advisor) would probably give me a subject and see that I am done in 3–4 years. "Independent" sounded great. Who doesn't like to be independent? I decided to give it a try.

Maybe there's a glitch in the matrix

At the time I did not realize that the average PhD process in Helsinki University of Technology took roughly 10 years (I have looked at a graduation book I have from my ceremony, in which people's starting and finishing dates are listed, I tried to calculate an average and arrived at 9.5 years). Not only those who finished took fairly long, but from among the PhD students I've met during my stay in Finland, quite a few have never finished. Those who did not finish, I must tell you, were not incompetent or lazy – in fact some are world-class researchers and very skilled people. Some perhaps placed the bar too high and perhaps could not judge just how original (and how significant) their work has to be. Possibly there were no explicit mechanisms that assured them that setbacks are to be expected in research projects, especially in such long-term ones as a PhD project. It seemed that people were expected to do their PhDs pretty much *all* on their own. The advising mechanism did not involve any structural support (no scheduled meetings, no graduate school guidance, no progress checks). One can view this as a good thing – why should a grown up in their mid- or late 20s or even early 30s should not be able to work all on their own? If someone is given *too much* mentoring that can be bad for his or her professional and personal growth.

However, lack of feedback can be hard, even for complete grown-ups. Organizational structures for making people feel supported, *explicit* mechanisms to discuss the PhD student's progress/work, and most importantly some frame that actually allows them not over- or underestimate the PhD process were nearly non-existent at the time. The struggle (that comes with having no feedback) is not specific to foreigners or only those of us who come from more communal societies – some locals (Finns) also have not completed their degrees (and the length of the PhD is not shorter for the locals).

Regardless of where you are, doing a PhD is (almost) always hard – just imagine that you need to stay interested/motivated and productive in a project that lasts forever without tangible intermediate results[16]. But I think the Finnish graduate students had it a little harder - if some structured guidance is offered. Last I know, such efforts were underway through a *graduate school*, and I think that is a very positive development.

---

16 Or check the PhD comics: http://phdcomics.com/comics.php

While we did not have a graduate school in place when I studied, I was very lucky with my financial situation, on and off I had scholarships and I worked 50% as a teaching assistant (TA) under fairly long contracts (at the Cartography and Geoinformatics Lab, as it was called back then –my 'minor' subject was in this area - I was doing my PhD with another group which was called Photogrammetry and Remote Sensing Lab).

When I look back I realize that I could benefit from simply having more information. For example, in Switzerland (at least in my current department) as well as in some other countries, PhD students structured guidance through a *graduate school* – where they get structured exposure/guidance to academic life from all kinds of aspects from qualified/experienced people. They are offered soft/transferrable skills; how to apply for a job, what does a good CV look like, how is an interview process for a professorial position carried out, what kind of paths are possible after you finish your PhD, etc., include scientific writing, 'critical thinking', project management, time management and similar. These courses are not all obligatory, and to be fair, some of which were available also in Finland (I did, for example, an elective scientific writing course, as well as an "intercultural communication" workshop). Being in courses through graduate school allows the students to be in the same room with the cohort of PhD students who started at the same time in the same department. They learn what it takes to do a PhD, talk to their peers and put their own project in perspective as well as their expectations from their advisors and themselves. This system does not necessarily produce *better* science, but it appears (to me) that it may be preventing some time loss. From a completely philosophical point of view, you might as yourself exactly what is "time loss" – one could say it's not "loss" at all if it's spent learning, trying your hand on unknowns and experimenting. I guess we should try to establish if people are happily exploring/experimenting or if they are in fact entirely lost and not discovering, and eventually quitting.

Back in Helsinki and back then, in my particular university and in my particular department, PhD students were treated like independent researchers who were in charge of their own projects (not like students or researcher in training). This was indicated in many legal details, university didn't treat us as students - e.g. our business cards (yes, we had business cards) read *Research Scientist* (instead of, for example, *PhD Candidate*) – and we were not granted students' cards by the university. On the other hand, the state treated us as students and not employees, in terms of our legal rights, which meant that we couldn't accumulate the legal rights of people who worked and paid their taxes (incorrectly so, because almost all of us did work and paid taxes). This induced extra paperwork, as year after year we needed to go to what was aptly called *Alien's Office,* and kindly asked if we could still stay another year because well, we were *still* doing our PhD (my friends in the UK at the time received three-year permits upon starting a PhD, which seemed to make more sense to me as I do not know anyone who finished the PhD in the first year) and still worked on the same job, essentially employed by the government.

Are PhD students really students, or are they researchers? I suppose they are somewhere in between, they are the backbone of research, but they are still in training (which is what creates the legal confusion). Most PhD students (while grown-ups), lack proper academic or any other professional experience as they start. This is exactly why they are supposed to be guided (not micro-managed, but guided while maintaining their independence). Perhaps isolating them is not the ultimate test to see if someone is worthy of a PhD.[17]

Intercultural communication class

Obviously, individual experiences are colored with ... well, the individual's background, and the individuals that we encounter. The 'isolation' experience was surely not the same (or to the same degree) for everyone. I was a bit between groups, and well, apparently I didn't speak the language (just understanding a bit of information that is posted around can go a long way sometimes) and maybe the way I was socialized wasn't helping with the Finnish 'ways' (e.g. cultural differences). A prime cultural difference example has been the *communication style* (a very common observation by any adult migrant, by the way, not unique to Finland at all). For example, offering information about yourself is a recipe for small talk back 'home' (perhaps similarly to other Mediterranean cultures, as well as the USA – because direct questions can sound like interrogation), and small talk is sort of a 'trust building' stage. In Finland (where small-talk seems to be largely omitted, I suppose trust is assumed?), talking about yourself might seem obnoxiously self-centered, thus might come across arrogant. Switching to the opposite perspective, seeming 'unwillingness' of the Nordic folk to engage into a conversation can be understood as arrogance (what's wrong in one culture is exactly what's right in another). The reactions are sometimes so subtle (at even major news) that it is hard to 'read' if the person could not care less, dislikes the situation, or approves something wholeheartedly.

---

17 There's a Nordic joke: You take a young promising candidate, place the person in a cell, give them water and food for five years. When you open the door, if there is a manuscript next to them, they were worth the PhD, if not, then not.

Once my Finnish (language) teacher said, if you say good morning to your colleague and they do not respond, you shouldn't take it personally – that an 'uninvited greeting' can seem offensive to people (invading personal space). This was a fresh perspective – it never occurred to me that saying good morning could be offensive – but experienced several versions of it. I arrive at the university restaurant, the person who works next door arrives right after me, we queue together and chat a little. I take my tray, go sit at a table, my co-worker whom I just chatted with, goes and sits at another table. I can't help but approach him and wonder out loud: "I hope I didn't say anything wrong?" He says, "No, I just didn't want to assume you'd want company". Eventually, I learned not to take these things personally but found my experiences curious/challenging enough that I needed an explanation and took an intercultural communication class to try to get a sense of how to behave in this new culture.

Let's see what I remember from this class: The *personal space was very important*. Check. I once tried to pick up a feather from a co-worker's pullover (we are both female, just to note) as we were chatting and she stepped back startled (her face seemed to say "what's your hand doing in my personal space!"). This surprised me as much as it puzzled her. In the context of personal space (from a Finnish perspective, that is), I learned a trick in the class: If someone comes too close, instead of facing he person, you can 'side them' thus when you move away from the person and they come closer, you go in circles and not get your back against the wall or out of the room (it can be a useful strategy!).

Any form of touching was pretty much foreplay. Check. I was told I was flirting with everyone, because I did the two-air-kisses-on-the-cheek thing with people (before I knew better). Oh also, people didn't shake hands, because that was perceived as 'very formal'. If you're lucky you got eye contact and a 'moi!' as a form of greeting. Sometimes that didn't happen either, and occasionally someone would disappear from the group without saying a word, I had to fight my urge to go after this person to see if everything is alright (because, as I grew up, this would be a sign of being offended).

Dialogues did not really work as dialogues but as pieces of monologues and you needed to pause and wait after finishing what you had to say, people weren't going to comment in between the lines (interruption is considered impolite). If you don't pause long enough people might keep waiting until you 'finish' – and this essentially could mean that you talk all the time. Check. We're at a conference in Beijing, roughly nine Finns and myself sitting around a table. A Turkish colleague approaches and wants to sit with us, "of course" I say. After minutes of him talking and no one in the group saying a word but me, he leans to me and whispers "did I interrupt something or did I say something offensive?" – neither was the case. He just didn't know to wait 'long enough' after he made his point.

The *Finnish society was more 'female' than 'male'* (I'll let the gender stereotyping go, but I'm well aware of it). This meant that the entire *culture was geared to protect the weak and not celebrate the winners.* Check. People are embarrassed from their successes, or at least they are supposed to be. Modesty is a big deal, and goes as far as not using the titles you collected anywhere – if a pupil is the 'best in class', you will keep that quiet not to make the others feel bad. This was another fresh perspective for me, I never thought of it that way, success was just something to aspire to in the way I was raised and you would celebrate success of others, or of yourself.

Males and females didn't necessarily socialized one on one, i.e. if two people were alone at lunch or at a movie, it was always perceived as a 'date'. Check. My male co-workers would invite other males to events and not me. I speculated many reasons in my head – but my gender didn't occur to me as a possible reason. Later on, my female colleagues invited me out and not the guys, which is when I started to suspect (there were not many women in the group, so it took me a while).

I learned more stuff in this class, but did it help me at the workplace, I don't know. I think maybe it did a little. At some point my students were laughing at my jokes, which was a relief (the intercultural communication class told me that I should state that it's a joke before I make the joke, then people will laugh – still can't quite accept that as it takes away the element of surprise, but apparently classroom is not a place people expect jokes in). You can imagine that I established the reputation of a 'slightly strange person', as a student later told me upon joining us as an intern –in the beginning, I attempted a lot of absurd jokes to 'break the ice' in my small groups or other teaching, and met totally straight faces (it is a very awkward, self-doubt inducing experience).

Talking about interaction, yet another example (relevant to academic life) springs to my mind. When we had foreign visitors, we hosted them with *much* less rituals then in Turkey, or Switzerland. They were often left on their own, and we always told them they should not be surprised if no one asks questions after their talks. This was often the case, I suppose people were too worried to 'sound silly' or maybe take everyone's time if the question was not relevant for the others in the audience. Individuals would go and ask questions sometimes after the talk was over, but a proper "Q&A[18] session" wasn't really a thing.

The beauty of this 'loose interaction' is that there is often no micro-management, you take charge of your decisions, you learn from your own failure or success. The other side of the coin is that without feedback, especially when you're a young

---

18 Q & A: Question and answer – it's expected to take place after conference talks and similar.

researcher, you might not be able to judge how well you're doing. Now you can of course question whether ambition and success are defining things (and one should question these) and/or how we should define them[19] – but without *some* feedback from others, only a small percentage of people seem to find what they do 'meaningful'. I'm opening a can of worms here when I start talking about *meaning*, but really, think about everyone you know, and what they do – when do they feel satisfaction? Yes, completing a project (say, you're building a table), and seeing it finished will give you pleasure (internal motivation) and it's great but many of us find even bigger pleasure if we can share – show that table to someone and hear that they like it. Seeing it used by others, seeing that it *helps* someone, or that someone tells you that it's actually a good idea, or good design or that they'd like to learn how to do this from you – all of these are what give the work the extra meaning (external motivation), thus the motivation to go on with a 4–5 year long (or longer) project such as a PhD.

Karonkka

Overall, despite the lack of sunshine, I think Finland is a very nice country, populated with lots of very nice people; however, its graduate students could use some external motivation. Where this doesn't occur naturally, some structure that will enforce a little bit of this could help people a great deal getting their PhDs in half the time. As I understand, a *graduate school* has been established soon after I left, and I believe, such efforts could save time, money and, also, some unnecessary grief.

Now, away from it for a long time, I get to enjoy the occasional visit and worry about some people who were already in their 8th, 7th, 6th, or 3rd year of the PhD when I left. Come on guys, finish that project and invite me for your *karonkka*[20].

---

19 See Alain De Botton's "kinder, gentler philosophy of success" http://www.ted.com/talks/alain_de_botton_a_kinder_gentler_philosophy_of_success.html
20 The elaborate Finnish PhD dinner party that is almost like a wedding. Invitations are sent, tables are arranged, there's a dress code, speeches, the whole nine yard. The defense process in Finland is also very ritualistic (ok, I've also seen a Dutch one, the Finnish one lacks the swords), in Switzerland it's much more casual.

The Technical University of Helsinki and its Doctoral Education

Jukka M. Krisp

As a short introduction some facts: I finished my doctoral degree at the Faculty of Surveying, at that time the oldest Faculty at the Helsinki University of Technology (TKK, *Teknillinen korkeakoulu*). The sub-department I did my research in was the unit of Cartography & Geoinformatics. I completed the degree in 2006.

Now, in 2013, the situation within my former Finnish university, within the faculty and the department, has changed dramatically over the last few years. I cannot elaborate on all the details, as I did pay only remote attention from abroad to what was and is going on. At some point the faculty (TKK, Faculty of Surveying) ceased to exist; nowadays, its units are distributed among other schools. Even the university does not exist anymore in its old form. It has merged with two other universities and changed the name to Aalto University. All of this makes it rather difficult to explain from where I graduated, even though the university has a history dating back to 1849. There is extensive information on the university's history and the organizational changes available[1], and to some extent this also affects the situation on current and future doctoral researchers within this university. Therefore my experiences may be partly outdated at this point. Moreover, I am somewhat irritated why the university had to change its name. This makes it difficult for national and especially international researchers, as they always need to explain that the university mentioned on their degree certificates has meanwhile been renamed from "TKK" to "Aalto", but it in fact is the same one.

How about the larger-scale educational setting for PhD candidates in Finland? Finland is a country that appreciates education. This is not necessarily meant in a financial way, but education is seen as a public responsibility. Therefore schools and universities are publically funded. This has advantages and disadvantages, but to elaborate on these is connected to society and politics and would exceed the scope of this essay. For PhD researchers who decide to stay within a university career, this narrows the perspective down to one point: you will most likely not get rich having chosen this career path. This has to be clear from the beginning and is to some extent valid for all publically funded research positions, also in

---

1 History and the organizational changes at the Aalto University are for example documented on the Universities webpage - http://www.aalto.fi/en/about/history/tkk/ (03/2013).

other countries. If you are after money in the first place, it may be the wrong way to pursue a doctoral degree.

There may be another observation to be made: In Finland, a person is not necessarily very well respected or appreciated just because of a very high educational level. Professors or doctors are part of a very equal society with flat hierarchies. Unlike in other countries (for example in Austria) titles as *Prof.*, *Dr.*, etc., are not very often used in Finland. They exist, but in everyday as well as in working life, they do not have any significant role. This is also reflected by comparably rather flat hierarchical structures within the universities, technical universities in particular. For PhD candidates, this means that generally, supervisors, other professors, even the chancellors, deans or rectors are somewhat easy to reach and to approach. There may be no need to do so, and it should be only done with a very concrete reason, but the flat hierarchies are something to be regarded as very positive.

To start a PhD in Finland is fairly easy. It requires a basically a "very good" or "good" MA or diploma degree and a PhD supervisor. That is usually a professor you contact before and see if he or she is willing and has time and commitment to act as your supervisor. Additionally, it requires a formal acceptation by the Faculty Board; in some cases the previous educational records are checked. The process is reasonably bureaucratic; eventually the supervisor is the bottleneck and is the most important actor in this process. The systems in Finland is slowly changing, a doctoral degree is not necessarily a "lifetime work". The "old" licentiate degree, a degree usually completed two or three years after the MA or Dipl. Degree, is not a requirement to pursue a doctoral degree. As a side comment: the German "Habilitation" does not exist in this form in Finland, so with a doctoral degree (and a good publishing record) you may formally qualify for a Professor position.

Why choose a Finnish University to pursue a doctoral degree? To start these thoughts off: Why did I end up at the Helsinki University of Technology (TKK, now Aalto University)? No particular reason I would remember in particular. I had not heard a lot about this university before. University ranking lists and evaluations/accreditations were not as important and popular in the late 90ies as they are now. I decided to follow a doctoral degree after finishing my MA diploma at the University of Turku, and decided to move from Turku to Helsinki. Within Finland, there is a very limited choice of doing research in the field of Cartography & Geoinformatics. And now, in 2013, it is hardly possible to intensively study and do research within this field in Finland anymore as a stand-alone program.

Why would someone else (from outside Finland) decide to pursue a doctoral degree at a university in Finland? This is a question that is impossible to answer. It seems that there are not too many rational reasons to do so. As a somewhat unrealistic example, a non-Finnish "high-potential" graduate, with unlimited funds, who decides to go for a doctoral degree in a foreign country, will probably have a US Ivy League university in mind as his/her first choice. The fuzzy definition of a "high-potential" or "a brightest mind" is related to this choice. Is the person a "brightest mind" and therefore can start his PhD research at Harvard, MIT etc., or the person starts there and therefore he/she is now one of the "brightest minds"? Unfortunately, on an international level, this "hen or egg sort of thought" does not apply to universities in Finland (at least at this point in time). When following an international career, a doctoral degree from Finland is an unclear choice, because within international applications, the human resource teams work the same way. They consult the (internal and external) ranking lists and some international assessment center scores. The larger Finnish universities, i.e. the University of Helsinki and Aalto University, appear in these lists with varying success. I will not cite the ranking lists here; it has been done too often in this kind of essays. In the end, these ranking lists are criticized by many authorities and for many reasons, so perhaps not too much attention should be given to these kinds of rankings in the present contribution.

Perhaps doctoral students who end up in Finland have other reasons than a straightforward career. They do not pursue an obvious choice, for example to follow the international ranking lists and apply their way down. Therefore international doctoral students who start their research at a university in Finland are the "brightest minds" of them all? That is probably not the case, but to some extent many of them have an "adventure genome", some of them have an attachment to Finland via the family, others may have a boyfriend/girlfriend (husband/wife) in Finland and need something to do. This last point is interesting, as the idea of dual career services within the university are restricted to new professors or researchers coming from abroad (or as the universities like to state, "they are recruited among the brightest minds in Europe and world-wide"). In practice it may turn out that the international husband or wife of successfully established persons in Finland end up at the university, because they need something to do. That does not necessarily imply that they are not the right choice for the university's research environment. In case their marriage makes them financially independent, they even have one of the most important requirements fulfilled. I elaborate on this a bit later in this essay.

What about the Finnish language for foreign PhD candidates? The Finnish language is difficult to learn. In my case it did not tackle the production of the doctoral work. Generally it can be a handicap concerning the everyday life for international PhD researchers in Finland, but this should not come as a surprise. PhD candidates deal with this language barrier in different ways. Some ignore

Finnish altogether and decide there is no point in learning it. Some others start to learn it for fun and experience. Some make more of an effort and come to a level to follow and participate in coffee meetings and to some extent in work-meetings as well. Very few eventually learn it up to a research and teaching level.

To start and finish a doctoral degree at a technical university, the Finnish language is not essential. English is accepted and used as the main working language. Still, to some extent, especially if the candidate is the only foreigner in the department's team, the work environment can be frustrating after some initial excitement. Foreigners tend to build international islands, cross-disciplinary as well as cross-departmental. This is partly because of the cultural/work situation and partly because of the language.

Teaching in the University as a PhD candidate

I was involved in teaching throughout my PhD candidate times. Now I am of the opinion that in most cases all the PhD candidates should be involved in teaching as well. A PhD candidate should at least supervise one full course independently, including the lectures, exercises, exams, the grading and dealing with the complaints about the grading from the students. It has a learning effect for the students and for the candidate and it is part of the job. In Finland, in most cases teaching is a pleasant experience (in Germany as well). The students are somewhat motivated, intelligent; the courses were small (at least in our TKK department of Cartography and Geoinformatics). It is not easy to generalize the teaching experiences accumulated in Finland compared to those in Germany, perhaps overall (this is to state a stereotype), the Finnish students were more quiet and shy.

Changes in the Research & Teaching Environment Due to Technology

Especially in the Engineering Sciences, we see a change in the educational system due to technological advances. In the Finnish universities, during the last years many attempts to establish some sort of e-learning platforms have been established with varying success. Still, efforts are developing and US-based platforms like Coursera[2] and others seem to contribute to the learning effect of students all over the world. For international PhD researchers who are involved in teaching,

---

2   E-learning plattform Coursera - https://www.coursera.org/ (access date 03/2013).

this is an interesting development. These platforms open the possibility to get involved in teaching, to some extent worldwide. As Finland used to be generally very positive in adapting technological advances, this may be an interesting improvement to follow.

The Helsinki University of Technology and the Money

Do I come from a rich university? I do not know about the objective financial situation of the TKK. During that time and also currently, it is perceived that the technical universities have the power, the positions and the money to make a big impact. From my impression, comparing the situation to other institutions, the general funding situation at the TKK was not a disaster. There seemed to be some funding for equipment (computers), travel (to visit conferences) and rooms (at least an "own" desk and phone). In the last years also project money could be applied for from several specific university funds. To summarize, it seems that a "temporary" and clearly defined purpose funding for equipment could be found or applied for via university specific funds. Also travel or equipment money seems to be reasonably possible to get.

Positions or more general, any money that would be spent on staff or salary was (and I believe still is) difficult. Personal research grants, which would secure a small income over 3 to 4 years were almost impossible to get. The postdoctoral researcher grants by the Academy of Finland are extremely competitive and not an option to rely upon too strongly, since about only five to ten percent of all applications are successful (the numbers may differ in details).

It is a strong point that the Finnish society in general values education on every level, not necessarily through providing money, but education is an important part of society. Therefore, the society may want to and will support a state-based university system and to some extent also support doctoral researchers. As to a large extent Finland maintains a state-funded system there is a danger of having an over-administration in distributing the limited funding. That is understandable, as the ones spending public money have to justify their way of spending these funds. It does not help in increasing the funding for the somewhat vague field of financing doctoral researchers. Thinking further, most of these doctors also would like to have adequate positions to work after they finish their projects. The balance of educating "new" doctors and professors and the available positions is difficult, if not impossible to determine. The technology, work environment, economy etc. is too dynamic for universities or ministries to plan this kind of balance properly.

Therefore the "dream" of being asked to stay at a permanent position at the university after finishing the doctoral degree was and is completely unrealistic.

From "old-time" stories (perhaps during the 60ies and 70ies?) there had apparently been times when top-level doctors of engineering had been asked, if they could picture themselves working in the university and had been offered a proper position to do so. This did not happen in the early years around 2000.

There is a story, if I remember right told by some professor (from physics?), who said to master students close to graduation, "If you would like to pursue a career in science and go for a doctoral degree, you should marry a dentist first". To some extent, this is good advice. The Finnish university system favors independent scholars, who are financially secure. If you are in the lucky position that there are many funding sources that will provide you with "extra" purpose-bound money, for example for equipment or visiting a conference, then you have the best basis to start from.

When it comes to money, the Technical University has attempted to use management or business processes within the somewhat unstructured university environment. That, however, seems to be difficult, and in some cases counterproductive. The university should be about the individuals working or studying there, and to find appropriate measures to value ideas or productivity appears to be complicated. Consequently, it is complicated to prepare clear cost-benefit balance sheets for a university environment. Applied to the context of this essay, how is it possible to prepare a cost-benefit balance calculation for a doctoral researcher? It is requested in many project applications, sometimes formulated in differing wordings or ways, but the supervisor and the PhD candidate are confronted with these thoughts.

A Snapshot Comparison to the current German system

How about the general PhD researcher's situation in Germany? Is somewhat better in Germany than in Finland? As Germany has a federal university system, every state (*"Bundesland"*) decides on their educational and research framework individually. There is no general answer to these questions. Perhaps based on the cultural and historical setting of German technical Universities, there seems to be a tendency to first have the project (with funding) or a fixed-term scholarship, and only then employ the PhD researcher. In many cases the position is split into two half-time positions, as PhD researchers will work full-time anyway. This seems unfair, but eventually it is a clear-cut deal. Take the position (or half-time position) for a fixed term, usually three years plus an additional option of up to one extra year, or leave it. The candidate can decide on that and the income or scholarship money is usually independent from the supervisors (professor's) goodwill. In case the candidate takes up the position, the money is available to the candidate. Once a contract is established or the salary (or scholarship) is granted, the PhD researcher can be reasonably safe to have a basic income, unless the performance is terribly bad, but this would be a somewhat special case.

For the practical process, especially concerning international students, the bureaucracy in Germany may be frustrating. In that respect (even if claimed differently in the last years) German universities to not have a service culture for their employees. International PhD researchers may be surprised by the amount of forms they have to fill in, acquire, translate, certify, resubmit etc., and this will apparently not change at any point in time. It is possible, with some level of frustration, to deal with these bureaucratic acts. Eventually these can be solved as well. As a side suggestion to PhD researchers who are about to start, for every paper there needs to be a signature and a stamp. So if you happen to have all documents copied, translated, etc. make sure there is a signature and a stamp from the issuing authority on them.

What happens after the PhD is finished?

In case you are an international PhD researcher in Finland and you are about to finish your PhD degree in the upcoming year, I urgently advise you to start looking for something that you may continue with after you are done with this degree. And start looking now.

I am not aware of any case in which a Finnish (the same is true for German) institution asked a finished international PhD student to stay at the university and continue to work there under "normal" conditions, that means a full-time continuing life time contract on an appropriate position with a proper salary. In other words, once you have done your duty, in this case finished your PhD degree, you are free to leave. Or to put it more bluntly, you should leave. In case you would like to have a full position in the university, expect a very long and hard way in front of you. International researchers especially have a difficult time to deal with this. After a finished PhD degree, these "international top-level researchers" (as some see themselves) expect to be "wanted" or "hunted" by the Finnish research institutions, companies or the universities. This is not the case, also not in the technical sciences (with some very rare exceptions). It is claimed by the media, that Finland needs more high-tech experts, engineers on the research level and in the universities. Universities claim to be "hunting" for the brightest researcher's on a worldwide level. In the end, what counts for an international PhD student in Finland with high qualifications, is that appropriate positions are also leveled higher; therefore "the air is thinner". There may be very few positions in this expert field and competition is very stiff. And, if you have nothing to offer, nothing will be offered to you in turn. Once you are wanted, it is easier. Once you have the opportunity for a professorship or a similar high-level research position, other options may likely arise as well.

Are there objective indicators of how "easy" it is to pursue a research career with a tenured position, after completing a doctoral degree in Finland? What about the statistics? The 2012 Aalto University Report states "95 of the 199 tenure track position allocated to focus areas were filled by the end of 2012. Of all appointed tenure track professors, 30% are from outside Finland, and 20% of them are women. The tenure track attracted international attention also in 2012: 73% of applicants were non-Finnish." (Aalto Annual Report 2012). We can also read in this report that 1519 doctoral degrees where completed in 2012, at Aalto University alone (Aalto Annual Report 2012).

To roughly summarize: "Year 2012 - ~95 positions at Aalto – ~1500 degrees only from Aalto" - it does feel highly competitive. Still, as statistics are usually given for the whole university or on national/country level, it is very difficult to make universal statements based on them. The different "habits" and practices within different subjects and institutes differ too much. It is not necessarily true that within engineering or natural science subjects, it is easier (or more safe) to pursue a university career than in the Humanities. It depends on the local circumstances, the research environment, the personal flexibility and luck, among other factors.

Is it different in Germany? Apparently not. When it comes to work perspectives or a safe (i.e. tenured) job, the universities are a rough environment. They are very insecure, highly competitive, and a bureaucratic nightmare. One difference may be that in Germany this is communicated better to the international PhD researchers. As many PhD candidates in Germany have a financially reasonable contract as they start, they also know that after four years this will end, no matter what. The pressure is realistically high from the start to think about the future. In Finland this situation used to be as rough or even rougher from the start, but this is not clearly stated to the PhD candidates upon their enrolment.

Following up on the TKK, now Aalto University

As I have mentioned previously, why the name change from "TKK" to "Aalto"? I suppose there are a number of good reasons for this, maybe stating "a fresh start?", "a break with traditions?", or "to stress the merger with to other very good universities?", etc. I do not elaborate on the politics or reasons for that, but I point out that it does cause some explanations especially for the international students and researchers who have a different university name stated on their certificate. In my personal case, this could be solved rather easily with some explanations and a link to the updated Aalto website.

When writing this short chapter about my alma mater, now the Aalto University, I got curious and will subsequently start to elaborate on the current situation at this university, not in depth, but a short, very incomprehensive survey. It seems that the university is strongly working on an international profile. The recent report available, i.e. the 2012 report, states a vision and I quote "The best connect and succeed at Aalto University, an institution internationally recognised for the impact of its science, art, and learning."[3]. By the way, to some extent, this overall vision seems to have a somewhat unclear grammar. I suppose it would be the "best connected University", while the term "succeed" seems to be unclear in this context. One level below, the goal of Aalto University is to be "A world-class university by 2020" (Aalto Annual Report 2012)[4]. The term "world-class university" is not defined in more detail.

The Aalto report is filled with the current buzz-words (research excellence, pioneering, competitiveness, leadership, internationalization, passion, freedom, etc.) used in university reports throughout the world. No surprise is encountered in this respect, since many universities follow the strategy of marketing themselves as the elite universities of the world. The University of Helsinki seems to follow a similar path. It seems university administrations take on the duty to create a vision for the university as a whole. This seems to be a new development. It is difficult to predict whether this will or does effect the situation of the international PhD candidates directly or indirectly, and if this development can be perceived as positive or negative.

To some extent it was (I believe still is) a mandatory requirement for current PhD researchers, as for all other university employees (regardless of research or administrative affiliation), to keep track and keep detailed records of their progress, publication activities, prizes, third-party funding etc., and report them to some university database (this applies even to your grand total of 1600 annual working hours, which you have to schedule in advance and eventually report; cynically enough, excessive working hours cannot be reported or taken into consideration since the reporting software limits you to 1600 hours). Eventually the university needs some records to prove why they are so excellent. In some cases

---

3   Quote taken from the Aalto Annual Report 2012, page 7.
4   Quote taken from the Aalto Annual Report 2012, page 7.

this may have a positive effect as successful activities are more visible throughout the university and to the research community as a whole. In other cases this may be seen as a "measure" for success. I would like to slightly specify this point by stating that it enables some administrative body to plot "performance curves" for PhD candidates, as well as for all other employees as well. This is time away from the lab or research-related work.

The general framework of ranking lists, measures of performance (like publications, third-party funding etc.) are becoming more important, which may be a disadvantage for Finnish researchers. To some extent Finnish research mentality is "down to earth", meaning "you should just publish or present something if you have something significant to say". For the research community this attitude is very valuable (especially in the technical sciences), but it is not necessarily supported or recognized in international ranking lists. The "publish or perish" attitude of the research community has reached Finland already some time ago and all PhD candidates have to take part in this. For international researchers this may be especially significant, as they may have greater difficulties to step out of a research career in Finland and find something else than well-connected local PhD candidates.

How does it continue? Do the Universities in Finland change further when it comes to PhDs?

Do future PhD candidates enjoy the same freedom and support as the one before them? In this case, I state that we should not predict the future, but we build the future ourselves. All "young" researchers, professors and PhD candidates, I have met in the last year or so agree on the principle of freedom in research and teaching. And they are the ones deciding on how supervision, research and teaching will be done in practice. Bureaucracy has taken over some part of the university, but generally university administrations, politics and bureaucrats seem to be reasonable and overall, the doctoral researchers still enjoy sufficient freedom to follow a particular line in research. In some cases a more structured approach is beneficial, but there should always be the choice and the PhD should be an intensive research and teaching time, to which the candidate and the supervising professor commit. If they decide on an unstructured approach, it is their (mutual) decision. Professors should be able to decide independently who they accept (or reject) as their PhD candidates, and supervise them accordingly independently. Graduate schools for PhDs, lectures or courses for PhDs, may be very valuable, but they should be optional. However, as this dynamic environment develops, PhD candidates have proven to be very flexible and they will adapt or transform the system to the diverse individual needs.

How to conclude?

How to conclude this short essay on experiences on being a PhD researcher in Finland? Generally, the tone set is positive. With some distance to the TKK in space and time, the tendency of "the grass is always greener on the other side" fades. As I can only elaborate, somewhat narrow-mindedly, on my experiences in the department of Cartography and Geoinformatics at a technical university, I have to conclude that it is, or better, was, an excellent place to finish a doctoral degree. As I try to be more general, I believe it is safe to say that the Finnish doctoral degree has a very high standard, to some extent too high, compared to other doctoral works accomplished in other universities worldwide. Having a very high quality doctoral degree is perceived as positive, but for more experiences international PhD researchers, who are generally well connected in their research field worldwide, it can also have a downside to it. They may feel that even though they have published so much, led successful research projects, taught many courses etc., but still have not finished or graduated, but this young fellow from the UK or China or elsewhere is already an (assistant) Professor?

In the end the research will be done, it does not really matter who does it, where it is done and how the framework for it looks like. Finnish universities, or more particularly, from my experience the TKK gathers students, researchers, professors and they perform top level research and teaching, no matter how the framework is set.

From Finland with Love – Recollections and Reflections of an Academic Emigrant

Andreas McKeough

One of the many advantages of the academic vocation is the freedom and mobility it offers. I, like many others, have taken advantage of this possibility and relocated my "doctoral enterprise" – that being my laptop and a pile of books – from Helsinki to Tartu, Southern-Estonia; a picturesque small town with a big university. A year ago, when I took this leap, I was in the third year of writing my doctoral dissertation in the University of Helsinki and in Folklore studies. The main reason for this move was not an academic one, but – as it is probably not hard to guess now – a romantic one. The change of scenery and to some degree lifestyle too, has, however, also been beneficial academically. In this essay, I will contemplate some of the differences of academic life and working culture in Finland and Estonia, based solely on my own experiences and thoughts related to them. These two countries are culturally very similar, and also their languages are closely related, but nonetheless many differences also prevail.

Firstly, let me look back at my time spent in Helsinki, where I spent most of my adult life, and reflect upon my studies, both as an undergraduate and a graduate student. I received my degree in Folklore studies, a discipline that in Finland originally centered mostly on the research of folk poetry, but has since become a theoretically and empirically broad discipline for cultural studies. As an undergraduate student at the University of Helsinki, I never had any worries about my studies or my future: I enjoyed studying and wasn't really at all concerned about the prospects of the discipline or entering working life – partly out of easygoingness, partly out of naivety. Maybe this was also due to the fact that in the last years of my studies, a time of taking big exams and writing my master's thesis, it had slowly dawned to me that I want to continue in the academic world and to scrutinize my topic – first-person narratives which describe the Finnish Civil War of 1918 – further in the form of a doctoral dissertation.

As I had my mind set up, starting life as a graduate student was not very difficult. A great help was also that the supervisor of my master's thesis encouraged me to pursue my academic ambitions. Therefore, enrolling in the graduate program felt easy, simply as the right thing to do. And easy it was indeed in other ways too: I just had to fill in a form and wait for acceptance, which is usually not denied from the students who want to continue their ventures after their master's degree. It can be a bit more complicated if there are too many applicants, in which case good grades come in handy. In my case, however, even though I was on the safe side with my grades, it never came to that, as there had been a few years without any new graduate students within the department of Folklore studies.

As mentioned, in my department and also generally in Finland enrolling in the graduate program is not very difficult. But finding funding for one's doctoral dissertation can be, as in Finland a large amount of graduate students are emitted into the program yearly, but then they are pretty much left to their own devices, at least in terms of finding funding. Funding is usually granted by various organizations and foundations, which have various 1–3 year programs for the funding of young researchers. However, the number of applications is vast and therefore the completion for monetary resources is quite fierce. And naturally receiving the first grant is the most difficult task, as life gets slightly easier once you have your foot in the door. I was very lucky to receive funding – if only for a year – relatively quick, some 3 months after entering the graduate program.

After receiving my first grant I started to work on my dissertation full of zest and zeal – and naivety – so typical to a newbie. I had a little, however in all ways sufficient, work space, half a room, in the department of Folklore, conveniently located in the middle of the City Centre Campus of the university; as central as can be and surrounded mostly by university buildings, like the biggest library. I immersed myself in writing, especially in the theoretic dimensions of my research. This was also a time of getting to know – and to befriend most, bless them! – my colleagues, whom of most were also toiling with their dissertation work, and some, like me, turning prematurely grey with theoretical and empirical ponderings. I really enjoyed being part of the graduate program and writing my thesis, as it was – and still is – very independent and creative work. And however lonesome I felt at times with my thoughts and thought processes, I knew that I could always ask my colleagues for help and opinion. Also the doctoral seminar, where people take turns to present their work, served as a valuable platform for comments and guidelines.

However, quite soon after starting my doctoral project things took a turn for the worse in the university, at least from the viewpoint of a doctoral candidate in Folklore studies. The reforming of the university, mainly the creation of bigger units, meant that resources for both graduate students and undergraduate students were cut, and an uncertainty settled in. For graduate students this meant that securing a work space at the university, even after receiving a hardly-fought grant, was no more imminent, actually quite the opposite. I was very lucky to be able to keep my little work space.

On the one hand these reforms and the uncertainty that followed brought some gloom to the atmosphere of our department, but on the other hand it also raised a fighting spirit – we shall not go down without a fight! – and made us graduate students and staff realize both the value of each other and of us as an academic group, the spearhead of folklore and also cultural studies in Finland. As we speak the fight has indeed not been lost, if not won either. Maybe the situation could be called a stalemate: resources were cut and the future of the discipline was very uncertain for a while, but the ball never stopped rolling, i.e. students coming in and going out, nor hopefully will in the near future.

In my second year within the graduate program I continued to research and problematize my topic. Only now, my funding came from the doctoral graduate school, which meant a slightly steadier life, if only for a year again. Most of this second year I spent writing, but also taking part in seminars and some conferences, and teaching one course (which I thoroughly enjoyed, even though it was a very practical one, mostly consisting of visiting different archives with the students). My work progressed, but not always in the right direction, especially theoretically. What I mean by this is that on several occasions I followed the wrong road, mainly tried to conceptualize psychological and cultural phenomena too broadly or in depth. Partly, this was due to my own stubbornness; of working all alone and mostly inside my head, the way I do like it, and of not communicating my thoughts to others or being in contact with my supervisors enough. However, this meant that the various seminars and conferences I presented my work at were of utmost importance, as were the comments of the audiences – consisting usually of more experienced scholars from my or nearby fields – they were extremely valuable for me, pointing me towards easier waters and challenging the necessity of too complex theorizing.

All in all I was, for the most of it, quite a happy camper most of the time that I spent in Finland toiling on my research. The biggest problem – for me personally but believe that I'm not alone here – was receiving funding three times in short term spells (I'm at the end of the third period at the moment). This means on the one hand a slight increase of stress, as you have no idea will you be able to continue your work the next year, and if you are then where and how. And on the other hand it means that quite a bit of your time is spent on writing funding applications and endlessly updating your research proposal. This does have one advantage though: you learn to market yourself – or rather your research topic. When I started to find my feet on the academic path, I indeed had no idea how valuable and important my research topic was! As sordid as it may sound, one does learn to market and advertise one's topic, to "sell" it to the funders, as most doctoral candidates rely on grants for their incomes.

So now I have reflected upon my experiences as a graduate student in Finland. To sum up, I enjoyed my work a great deal, and cannot say that the independence, even loneliness, of the work weighed me down. However, I wouldn't recommend the vocation to people who need other people around them and to work with, because – even though you have your colleagues – at the end of the day you are alone with your research. And in the worst case one might end up working from home, alone.

Even though I enjoyed working in Finland, coming over to Estonia was a very pleasant and inspirational change. Of course this is mostly due to the aforementioned romantic factor – home is where your heart is etc. But also in general I found the environment of a classic university town invigorating: a small, historical town with a big university and active student life – maybe best compared to Uppsala, Sweden, where I have also lived for a short while – is a good place to live as a graduate student too, as you are in no way out of place. Also the smallness of the town means that it is easy to get around and you don't spend an hour a day on a bus stuck in a traffic jam.

When I first came over, I was a visiting doctoral student for a three-month spell. This meant getting to know the people at the local department of Folklore and getting to know the ropes in other ways, too. Immediately, I felt a good vibe at the university and the department too, and this feeling has not changed a bit in the year I have lived here. I felt very welcome from Day One, and also was enthralled by the warm atmosphere of the department. And by this I do not mean that the atmosphere in Helsinki would have been bad, on the contrary, it was very good, too. Actually it seems folklorists around the world, being the practitioners of a small discipline, seem to be quite a tightly knit pack, and to get along well both academically and personally. But here in the department in Tartu I just welt an extra notch of warmness and togetherness.

One important factor for this good atmosphere has in my opinion to do with a more easy-going mentality. Previously I had thought that the universities in Finland were pretty much the most informal in the world, with students calling their professors by first name and so on. However, I found this to be even more so the case here in Estonia, where the staff, graduate and undergraduate students – of the latter both the ones in bachelor's and master's programs – are on very friendly and jolly terms. The staff takes part in in the parties arranged by the students and the discussions on life and studies are lively and commence on equal terms. It is not a rare sight to see the professors at these parties, often also taking a sip from the introductory bottle circling around. This means that the students are used to interacting and talking to the staff, basically that they know them, which makes academic acquaintance and co-operation easier and more relaxed.

In Finland it seems, at least in our department, that there is more of a divide between the students and the staff and researchers of the department. Of course there is some interaction too, and especially the students who are in the later stages of their studies are known to the staff. But the students keep more to themselves, especially socially, and the parties they arrange are very rarely visited by the staff or the graduate students. I believe that the reason for this lies not so much in the people, knowing how friendly and warm my colleagues on the other side of the bay are, but more so in historical factors, which in this case account for things being more rigid in Helsinki. Luckily there seems to be a bit of a change coming to this, as both the students and staff have announced their desire for more discussion, which has led to the staff and students having coffee together now and then to discuss things of more or less academic nature. Partly, this change seemed to stem from all the reforms that were going on and the uncertainties surrounding them – difficult times call for a unified front.

Another upside of this quite "democratic" academic atmosphere within the Folklore department in Tartu is that it is academically very useful. The students take part in planning and arranging many seminars and conferences, which is very beneficial both for the staff and students: the staff gets much needed help in the midst of their workload, and the students gain valuable experience. At the same time both learn more about each other and how to work together. Also students, even ones in the bachelor's program, are regular speakers at these events, gaining again valuable experience, however terrifying it is to stand up on a platform in front of an audience and to talk about your research topic for the first time. In Finland, seminars and conferences – both arranging them and taking part – are mostly for graduate students. The students in Tartu, or more so, their organization, also publish an academic journal aimed both at graduate and undergraduate students. This is another good platform for presenting your research topic, and also for co-operation and acquaintance.

Another very positive thing I have to mention about studying in Estonia, very much initiated by the professor here in Folklore studies, is the large amount of visiting doctoral students from all around the world. This means getting to know colleagues from different universities and cultures, ones who are in the same stage of their lives and careers. It also is an opportunity for intriguing discussions, networking and simply for getting to know more of the world. Also it is very interesting to take part in seminars with such an international crowd. The doctoral seminar here is slightly different from Helsinki, where mostly people present their topics and discuss them, as here it is based on reading landmark texts and discussing them. Both styles have their advantages.

Also, one positive side of this international crowd is that it also offers a social network for people coming to Estonia from different countries. I haven't felt the importance of such a network so much, as I knew quite a bit of people through visiting here with students from Helsinki and from coming over several times when romantically engaged before actually moving here. However, I have noticed that Estonians have, to some degree, the same cultural behavior features as the Finns: locals, even though very friendly and welcoming, might appear slightly reserved, valuing their privacy and the space around them, and thus not the easiest people to befriend. But it seems that the upside of this is the same as in Finland: once you finally manage to befriend a local, it is honest and loyal friendship, one that might well last for your lifetime, even if life relocates you geographically somewhere else.

Otherwise, the academic life here is quite akin to the one in Helsinki, the students and graduate students have just about the same joys and sorrows. The funding system is a bit different here to my knowledge, but I will not touch that subject, as I am in no means an expert on it. Working here for me is quite the same as in Helsinki: independent, lonely and gray hair generating. I work at home and in the library mostly, sometimes also in some cafeteria downtown. As always, I work mostly in "bursts" – when I feel bewitched by inspiration and flow – but sometimes also toil intensely and stressfully for days and nights, usually before article and presentation deadlines and such. On the other hand, sometimes, when the brain is jammed and the inspiration gone, days pass and I get nothing done.

In these pages I have reflected upon working both in Finland and Estonia. I have pointed out some of the up- and some of the downsides of being a graduate student in these countries, within my field of studies, and of working on a doctoral dissertation. These reflections are mostly connected to my personal experiences and perceptions of them, so by no means I mean to generalize on behalf of them. I do want to add, that in my view being a graduate student is great: intellectually stimulating, creative and diverse, and you meet lots of interesting and nice people. No two days are exactly the same, as the process slowly moves ahead and your grey cells are challenged by new thoughts and stimulated by the thoughts and ways of thinking of other people. Also, I am relatively happy with the doctoral system in Finland: the competition for funding is tough, but on the other hand the threshold for entering the graduate program and for trying out whether it is your thing is rather low. And I have never minded the loneliness of the work, even though I can understand that for many it is not the ideal circumstance. However, the plans to reform the graduate program into doctoral schools seem promising, as it surely means more cooperation between the doctoral candidates and also a broader curriculum.

Also related to the aforementioned reflections, I have to confess that I do get slightly annoyed when some people complain how though it is being a doctoral student. Sure, it is demanding, difficult and even draining at times, and very independent. And the salaries or other compensations are not too great either, especially when they often also are of short term. But it is, or should at least be, one's of choice to venture in that world. And furthermore, while toiling away you are toiling towards a degree that will – or at least should – raise your value on the work market and open new doors.

Taking these points into consideration, I would not recommend graduate student life for anyone looking for easy (or even decent money), long-term jobs or wanting to get onto the top levels of society. There are other, far better ways for that. I see the research vocation as one that suits certain people; ones that have the calling and desire for it, and who probably are most useful for their societies in producing knowledge of our world and us human beings. Working in different environments and academic cultures is also a great as an experience, one that should be more common. In my view, there is not much difference between working in Finland or Estonia, but this is probably related also to the cultural similarities of these countries. However, I believe that working in Finland as a foreigner can be pretty demanding in some ways – of which the other authors of this book will probably be able to tell more. But I am sure that, even with these difficulties, people in the academic field usually can cope quite well, as I believe that the critical thinking that the vocation demands is usually accompanied with an open and curious mind.

Ambivalence, Cancer Narratives, and Passion

Piret Paal

On the day of my doctoral defense, the 15th of January, 2011, I began my *lectio praecursoria* with the following opening line: "Until today this has been an untold story. It is about to become my personal experience narrative that is a construct of various experiences, thoughts and feelings. This story – untold so far – has been my experience that I will interpret, here and now, to this particular audience, from my point of view." Unlike at the University of Helsinki, I am not in a position to guess who is going to read this story unfolding on following pages, but I am convinced that narratives have to be constructed in order to share our minds and to make the lived experiences meaningful. Hence, another untold story about me becoming a doctor of philosophy at the University of Helsinki shall be presented here.

The early years of my academic life

My academic journey began in 1995 at the University of Tartu. I became a philology student majoring in Estonian and comparative folklore and Estonian language. My choice was based on two criteria: folklore studies seemed more down to earth compared to literary studies, fitting my pragmatic nature, and the Estonian language presented a personal challenge, because to understand how a language really functions poses a true challenge. So far, both decisions have proved to be right, considering the following steps on my academic path. And therefore, I have to express my sincere regret that comparative folklore, which finally became my major field of studies and later also of my research, has distanced itself as a discipline from linguistics so gradually.

In 1997, I began to work as a research assistant at the Estonian Folklore Archive. This opportunity led me to defining my main research topics: narratives and illnesses. As I enjoyed the extensive access to a vast archival material, the theoretical framework to approach this data appeared somewhat indistinct. Thus, the opportunity presenting itself in spring 1999 to go to Turku as an Erasmus exchange student came just at the right time. In 1995, Prof. Annikki Kaivola-Bregenhøj had published her book on storytelling, which had strongly affected my theoretical understanding of narratives and their functioning, thus, becoming one of her students seemed like the right step. In September 1999 I officially became an Erasmus exchange student at the University of Turku.

I defended my baccalaureus thesis in the spring of 2000 and immediately applied for enrolment to the master's program at the University of Tartu. The place was granted, and after a year in Tartu I applied for another exchange period at the University of Helsinki. This decision was mainly connected with a research project that I was involved in at that time. However, one cannot deny the personal impression that "once you have slide out of your cozy homemade soup bowl" there is no sliding back, or, at least, it will not be easy. So, I studied at the University of Helsinki, was involved in a research project at the Kalevala Institute at the University of Turku lad by one of the most influential folklorists in the world, Prof. Lauri Honko, and continued my cooperation with the Estonian Literature Museum. It took me four years to finalize my master's thesis, but the opportunity to work in Helsinki allowed me to do comparative studies on ague (Nordic malaria) legends and ethnomedical healing practices in their most fundamental manners.

The beginning of my Doctoral Studies in Helsinki

In spring 2005 I applied for a PhD position at the University of Helsinki. To avoid any misinterpretations, I applied only for the right to be a doctoral student, which means there was no money involved. Having the PhD position at the University of Helsinki meant being granted with the university e-mail account, the right to use the library as well as the computer labs and enjoy the generous offer of 600 pages of free print offs per semester. That is about it. Anyhow, my first supervisor, the head of the folklore department, Prof. Anna-Leena Siikala, assured me that my research topic "Cancer patients' narratives" was promising enough in terms of finding some funding to complete my thesis. A scholarship is called *apuraha* in Finnish which literally means 'aid money'. So, there I had it - the PhD position, without any aid money.

I suppose I could have enjoyed a more intensive academic relationship with people working at the University of Helsinki if I would have been a part of some bigger research project or at least involved in some doctoral program financed by the Academy of Finland. However, the unfortunate truth is that until very recently, the field of ethnomedicine has hardly ever been a topic for some joint projects and the research outcomes within this field are often based on single researchers' interests and initiatives. When it comes to narrative studies, there was clearly a shift towards oral history taking place in Helsinki in the beginning and middle of the decade after 2000. Call me old-fashioned, but the oral history framework did not match my understanding of how (illness) narratives function in terms of sense-making and finding the meaning in bad health and suffering. So, also theoretically, I was and stayed loosed-laced until the very end of my doctoral saga.

Fortunately, I had some previous experiences in writing research project application and subsequently applying for grants. After I had found out which grants I could apply for, it happened so that my very first application turned out to be a success. Just an interesting fact, in 2006 approximately 8000 applicants applied for grants at this particular foundation and 800 (10%) were granted with some sum of money. In my opinion it was not only the important topic that made my application an outstanding one, but also the right recommendation letters from my supervisor in Helsinki and from the head of the folklore department at the University of Tartu. The research funding was granted for one year with an opportunity to re-apply for a funding of two more years.

Observing my fellow PhD students, I soon realized how devastating the never-ending application process can be. Some of them had been in this on-off circle for more than ten years, and several others still are today! The most terrible thing is, once you have the money, you get a place at the department where you can conduct your research and enjoy the academic conversations with your colleagues. I am fully aware that this is about far more than only the academic talk; it is also the moral, psychological and even spiritual support of your colleagues that keeps you going when "the suffering" is at its greatest. Anyhow, you are expected to pay 14% of overhead to the university to enjoy such adjustment. The second disadvantage, the research grant was until 2007/8 a non-taxable income, which leads to diminished social security in old age. The third rather inhumane aspect was and still is that immediately, when you are out of your research money, you are forced to give up your workplace and stop using the department facilities. Finally, getting to know the feeling that starts to nag you a couple of months before the money runs out led at least in my case to understanding that you cannot really concentrate on your research under such circumstances. Therefore, I decided that I cannot spend more than three years on completing my thesis, which naturally lead to some different kind of agony and somewhat unexpected alienation.

The days filled with passion

Working on my research materials and writing my doctoral was a passionate act. Passion (from the Latin verb *patī* meaning to suffer) refers to strong feelings that can be positive as well as negative. In German language the meaning becomes even more detailed, the word '*Leidenschaft*' stands for passion, but is put together from two verbs '*leiden*' (to suffer) and '*schaffen*' (to achieve/to create). From November 2006 until January 2011 I suffered, I achieved, and above all, I was entirely involved in my research. I really enjoyed my research project, yes indeed;

I was and still am passionate about this particular aspect of human life: living with an illness and making sense of it.

The positive part of working on a doctoral thesis that is not bound to a bigger project means that you can fully concentrate on doing your very own research. It is a time free from assistant duties, teaching, organizing seminars or conferences, dealing with bureaucracy or editing books and journals, this is all you can have, of course, unless you personally want it to be different. This means that a researcher actually has three full years in his or her service to conduct a single study and publish the results. The exceptionality of such a privileged situation becomes quite explicit after you are done with your thesis, because under normal circumstances scholars are faced with manifold tasks that have to be taken care of simultaneously. Of course it takes lots of self-discipline to organize your days so that every day is made meaningful and perceived as a step further.

Despite my loose connection to the university in general I enjoyed a very nice network of colleagues and friends around me. As I worked in the archive of Finnish Literary Society at Hallituskatu 1 I was physically close to the folklore department that was back then situated in Mariankatu 11. At Mariankatu 8 there was my old workingplace, the Finnish Society, where I had spent six month in 2002 as a Finnish language trainee. In the same building there were situated the Estonian Institute and the Tuglas association. So, my lunch breaks at the *Tiedekahvila* a few corners further served my longing after academic discussions, pep talks and just meeting some familiar faces entirely. But it would be dishonest to say that I did not miss the coffee breaks that for some reason have gained a very particular place in the Finnish work life.

In the autumn of 2007, I mostly worked from home, and then some weeks again in the library. If I think of this period I recall only back pain, which is natural if you carry around a laptop, a load of Xerox-copies and all these books that you might need during a long day. As an aftermath, even now my body reacts with repulsion even if I think about carrying around some bigger amounts of articles or other materials for research purposes. At that time my favorite work corner was in the Alexandria library cellar. The Alexandria Learning Center and Library is a very modern but at the same time cozy construction equipped with all kinds of high-tech facilities representing Finnish functionalism at its best.

Sometimes I sat down at the university coffee place and worked there. The folklore department had been moved to new rooms in Vuorikatu 3, so in the cafeteria I could, again, see and meet my colleagues occasionally passing by. From time to time I was invited to have lunch in the department's kitchen, until in the beginning of 2008, somewhat to my great surprise, I got my very own working place in the departments archive within the Topelia study-complex situated at Unioninkatu 3.

That was a huge relief, because I did not have to carry all the copies, notes and the computer with me anymore. I interpreted this advantage as a Finnish kind of acknowledgement (no words involved) to my personal dedication.

Teaching experience

Since 2004, I had worked as a freelance Estonian and Finnish teacher with several different groups, but I had no university level teaching experience yet. In 2008, my second supervisor, Dr. Mervi Naakka-Korhonen, asked me if I would like to give a lecture on folk medicine for medical and cultural studies students at the University of Turku. I thought of it as a nice challenge and agreed to do it. It marked the beginning of my interdisciplinary explorations between medicine and humanities that are still ongoing. I have to say that I found Finnish students very polite and cozy. Perhaps, except this one time, when they came to my seminar knitting! It was fairly easy to find a common language with the students. I assume my personal flavor back then was partly due to my Estonian accent that many Finns find somewhat "cute". In spring 2009 I gave a course on ethnomedicine. Again, the students were really active and showed lots of personal interest in the presented subject. I suppose it is not possible to compare Estonian, Finnish, and German students. However, it is my personal impression that the Finnish students were the best-prepared to read required literature or even challenging theoretical articles in other languages than their mother tongue. What Finnish students lack compared to German students are the presenting skills, which so falsely may give the impression of being unprepared and incompetent. What I miss while teaching in Germany is the opportunity to address the students with an informal *you* (*Du*), which in my opinion makes the learning and teaching milieu a lot more responsive. A thing to remember: in Finland you never interrupt your colleagues or students even if the pauses between unfinished speech acts last longer than 12 seconds.

Towards wrapping up

I moved to Germany in September 2008. Changing the country whilst preparing your thesis is not a very great idea. Moving in general tries your personal boundaries and borders, not to mention combining moving countries and finishing your thesis. Somehow, cut off from all social connections, I worked like a mad dog. The "so lame" social network *Facebook* kept me going during this challenging period. It created an impression of being connected and being part of some community, although in reality this community was only a phantom.

Until October 2009, I still enjoyed my scholarship. I also knew that being a foreigner living abroad I had no chances to apply for further funding from Finland. This meant I needed to wrap up my thesis. Between finishing the chapters I read the *Twilight* book series to clear my head and keep me sane. A chapter ready, check. Another *Twilight* book, check. There I was, first draft put together. Suddenly, my first supervisor's health condition got so bad that she stopped guiding all her doctoral students altogether. This naturally meant finding a new supervisor for several doctoral students, which was a challenge for a small department. For me personally it meant having no money, no supervisor, no social duties, no job – in other words: a huge amount of stress piling up. The uncertainty was eating me up. Finally, after three or four months, I got a new supervisor. Prof. Annikki Kaivola-Bregenhøj did her best to support and advise me, but she was a retired professor from another university. Of course, I am really grateful to her for her quiet and wise support and immense theoretical preparedness. But the thing is, besides the theoretical knowledge, a doctoral student needs also some practical support about how things are to be done at the particular university. So, a supervisor should be always part of the system, part of the university life, to be able to provide also some practical support. In my case, also my second supervisor was retired during the spring of 2010, so the already loose connection to the University of Helsinki became inexistent.

Good and bad things come in pairs. I was able to apply for a three months' scholarship to finish up my doctoral thesis (*väitöskirjanloppuunsaantiapuraha*). This is a fixed scholarship provided by the university. A very nice thing, however: the scholarship was granted in March and transferred to my bank account in June. Unfortunately I cannot recall what the exact reason was, but as I tried to inquire about the delay a funny and not at all untypical thing happened: I called the Faculty of Humanities and the phone rung like a really long time. I called once again; and again. Finally someone picked up, without introducing herself or saying hello. The only thing I heard was: "This person is currently not available" (*Tämä henkilö ei ole juuri nyt tavoitettavissa*), and the phone was hung up. I was not quite sure if it was a really a human being or a machine, but I assumed that talking was a hard deed for a Finnish bureaucrat.

On the 25th of May 2010, I submitted my thesis for the peer review. This happened after both of my supervisors and the chair of our department had mutually agreed that the work is ready to be submitted. And then I had to wait. Officially the reviewers have three months to provide their assessments. As it was the beginning of summer, unofficially it was clear that nothing will happen before the end of September. You see, part of the academic freedom for university employees in Finland is that the summer is for visiting conferences, doing fieldwork and taking a very long summer vacation. I personally find it very nice and rewarding, because then you can begin in September completely reloaded. Thus, while my colleagues got reloaded I had to wait. During the summer it was fine, but by the end of September there was still no decision. I sat behind my computer and pushed the refresh button of my inbox the whole day long. This lasted until the decision finally arrived: "I am allowed to defend my thesis!"

By that time I had understood that an academic career suits actually only those who are financially extremely well off. This statement was made even clearer during the following months. Suddenly, the University that I had had a very loose connection with posed a number of demands regarding my thesis: the work should be proofread by someone working at the university language centre, it should be published and free copies (60 back then when the thesis was published online, and 80 in case there was a print-only publication) should be given to our University library and additional free copies sent to some faculty members.

I paid the language check from my three months' scholarship. I did not use the university language centre services, because my usual proofreader was less expensive and our work relationship functioned well. However, the language centre was obliged to do the final language proof and give their official permission prior to publishing the thesis. My thesis was rejected twice by the language centre. Imagine the stress! As my proofreader asked for an official check list to meet the standard criteria the language centre was unable to provide it. I tried to keep myself out of it, but after the second rejection that ended with an encouraging "It is almost there!" I tried to get some advice from my department, how to handle the situation and the answer was: "Let the language centre do another check up!" When I asked: "Who is going to pay for the second proof reading?", I got an answer that the folklore department had no money, I should take time, let it be and see what happens. A good advice for someone who cannot afford being quite finished yet; however, that was not my case. So we, my proofreader and I, did not give up, submitted the thesis for a third time for the language check and finally got the permission to print.

For printing the thesis, the University admitted another 1000 euro of scholarship. I personally find that publishing the thesis prior to the defense is a quite unnecessary act – a waste of money, time and nerves. An online thesis should be enough at this point and a book could follow later if the defendant wishes so. It would give an opportunity to look for a good publishing house and for an experienced editor or an editorial team, who is able to advise the author to make the best of it. Nevertheless, compared to the book of which 60 of total 100 copies probably rot in some library cellar, the online version of my thesis has been currently downloaded 2034 times and cited in several publications all over the world, which I find quite remarkable.

One important act before the defense is selecting the opponents. The defendant is allowed to make suggestions who should be his or her opponents. At the same time it was made clear that the department has no money to fly in someone from the United States, Germany or some other city in Finland. In my case it would have only been fair to have an opponent from some other country than Finland for the sake of "seeing the big picture". Unfortunately that did not happen. And I just did not have the guts to stay in for my demand. I was actually asked if I would agree to do the defense in Finnish, which I interpreted as a compliment, but denied firmly.

The big day and the big night

The big day arrived on the 15th of January. I had booked the lecture hall, bought a black costume, did my hair already at 7.30 in the morning and was ready to march in front of the audience at 9 a.m. There was a one page long story about my thesis in *Hufvudstadsbladet*, the Swedish language daily newspaper, published in Helsinki, which indicates that a doctoral defense has a social significance in Finnish society.

The defense at the University of Helsinki is a very official and predetermined event. The *kustos*, chair of the department, opponents and defendant enter the hall. The "actors" become introduced and the "show" can begin. The *lectio praecursoria* may last approximately 20 minutes. Then the opponents give their general comments (standing) and after that begins the discussion (sitting). If the defense lasts longer than two hours there is a time for an official break. The overall suggestion is that the defense should not last longer than six hours. We had agreed not taking the break, although my defense lasted almost 4 hours (felt much longer).

I must admit that I do not remember much of this event, but some questions and comments were really interesting, particularly the "national" ones. For example: "Why did you not write your thesis in Finnish?" My research material was in Finnish. I considered it challenging enough. Writing in Estonian was not an option, because who could have been my supervisor in that case? Writing in Finnish? I thought about it, but I could have not done it without some extensive help. Plus I would have lost my available "dumb readers", English-speaking friends, who are extremely useful in terms of progress control. I also knew that Finland would not be the last place to end up on my journey, so it felt quite obvious that as an international researcher I also had to conduct my research in today's *lingua franca*. Have I regretted this decision? Not really. If I think about my current position, what could I do with a thesis in the Finnish language? Who, in Germany or some other country, except Finland or Estonia, could read it? This had to be said although I think writing in your own language is very important I also think it is a bit funny to expect it from some foreign researcher who temporarily is visiting your country. Writing in another language is a struggle in one way or another. Another striking, somewhat "nationalistic", comment I received considered the structure of my work. I had built my thesis up as a collection of case studies: chapter 1, chapter 2, and etc. One of my opponents told me: "We in Finland do not do it like this!" No further comment.

My defense was long, boring and colorless. I felt sorry for my supervisors and my audience for not making the defense livelier, friendlier and more interesting, but as the Finns always say, "it takes two to tango". So, I thanked all parties involved and we, four ladies in black, marched out again. Being out of this hall, in the arms of my friends I felt so relieved that I could not do anything else but cry.

In the evening I had invited my opponents, colleagues and supervisors to a traditional dinner party called *karonkka*. Even here I was capable of not following the Finnish rules, namely, I could not give my thank you speech. I just could not and of course I feel bad about it, but what can I do? I very much hope that people could read the gratitude from my cried-out eyes. All the nice words I heard! I was not prepared to take it in that night. Carstén Bregenhøj, a Danish folklorist settled in Finland, told "that I made history that day, but only foreigners can understand it fully". I certainly did go on with my own story at that point.

Looking back

Sometimes I think that it would be great to be a carpenter. I like wood work a lot. Sometimes I think I would like to be a writer or a journalist. I like to write, but I am afraid to open up myself. Sometimes I think I would like to be a teacher at school. Then again, I do not stand noise and repeating myself so much. Sometimes I would like to be a storyteller. Sometimes I think, what could I be instead of being a researcher? Honestly, I do not know and now apparently is too late to change my mind. But the nice thing about being an academic is that with your knowledge you can modify students like the carpenter modifies wood. You can write and argue objectively and subjectively without revealing much about yourself. You can teach, give advice and make suggestions, and in general, the students behave. You can tell great stories and if you are lucky these stories will be retold. Even if the academic life as a middle management research assistant is no honey licking it has its freedoms and great rewarding moments as well.

After what I have experienced, would I go to Helsinki and do my doctoral thesis again? No doubt, I would do it. Why? I am just so passionate about what I do and I like it that way.

Catching Rhythms of the Extended University Sphere

Tarmo Pikner

Slow, quick, quick, slow, ...this is the rhythm of the slow foxtrot dance, characterised as a smooth movement of walking. At first sight this dance seems easy. In regard to the quick steps, the slow ones happen to be more difficult to perform. It is the stretched lightness that makes these slow steps so challenging. Besides dance, various rhythms of practice are intrinsic parts of putting together one's doctoral thesis at any particular university. Here I employ the metaphor of rhythms (inspired by Lefebvre 2004/1992; Edensor 2010) to reflect on my personal experience of conducting doctoral thesis and research work in Finland. Social rhythms are intertwined with virtual and dominant rhythms forming wider spheres of the dissertation process. The five year time distance from being directly part of Finnish doctoral system enables me to see some aspects more clearly, and something is forgotten and in silence as well. The rhythmic sphere of the university and the dissertation involves many people, places, institutional issues, emotions – only some lines of the sphere can be discussed in this chapter.

Geography and a Few Lines of the Dissertation Sphere

The learning and practicing of academic 'geography' started for me at the University of Tartu in Estonia. This period was essential to become involved into this multi-sided sphere of knowledge and even lifestyle. The studies continued at the University of Turku in Finland with the master thesis at the Department of Geography. One-and-half year spent in Turku brought me together with some of the wonderful people writing in this book as well. After the Turku-period I worked in Estonia, and after some years moved to Germany with an applied research project. My proposal to start the doctoral thesis at the University of Oulu was accepted, and it was needed to move from crowded and intensive Ruhr area towards northern Finland. I was positively minded about the research project theme and people involved, but there were some doubts about the living environment in Oulu. These doubts concerned mostly the distance(s) related to the northern location of Oulu. Florida (2002) argues that highly educated professionals value a location's characters more than the particular work to be done in the situation of choosing residential countries and cities. According to my experiences, there are needed several compromises in balancing purposes and emotions related to the places of living.

My Oulu period and the dissertation work at the Department of Geography began in January 2004. It was winter, with short days and much snow - white quietness imprinted over environments with becoming associations, which introduced new people and things. I had to catch up, because my colleagues had enrolled already half a year earlier. It was part of a large scale research project focusing on regional innovation systems (financed by a public grant in 2004–2006). My research analysed the phenomenon of 'urban networks' in the cross-border context of the Baltic Sea area (Pikner 2008). The theoretical framework was elaborated through case studies including six cities/towns. The research project enabled me to take part in several international conferences as well. It was agreed upon in quite an early stage that the dissertation was to comprise four peer-reviewed articles and a broad synopsis. This way of composing the doctoral thesis has become more common in Finland, although some scholars at the department were rather critical about fragmentary aspects of an article-based dissertation compared with a monograph.

I found it useful to focus more intensively on the particular papers as part of the thesis. This was although each manuscript of each paper got partly rewritten in the review process and therefore there was additional effort needed to keep the dissertation acceptably coherent. It means that the sphere of dissertation included also anonymous journal referees who sometimes scared me as an inexperienced beginner with harsh criticism. Now it seems that there would have been more time needed to elaborate the article manuscripts before sending them into the review process, which sometimes can be very slow (in my experience from four months to one year). This way of working created slight frustration of being declined from swift publishing. On the other hand, the critical feedback enabled to test and to improve some approaches in rather early phases. However, it was possible to complete the thesis within five years in December 2008. The final phase of the thesis came along rather hectic because I already started to work as a researcher at Tallinn University besides preparing for the dissertation event in Oulu.

The University of Oulu was established in 1958. The university is a workplace for 3000 employees and 17000 students. The recruitment of foreign people started to increase after Finland joining in European Union in 1995. In 2006, more than 5% of the university employees had a foreign background, which is rather high in the Finnish context. The Internationality Plan aimed to double (up to 300) the number of foreign employees in period of 2005–2010 (Hautala 2011). It means that there were institutional intentions to accommodate initiatives involving researchers with culturally diverse backgrounds. My dissertation project was part of these tendencies in some way. The geography department at Oulu University had only one non-Finnish researcher (from Switzerland) in September 2003. The particular internationalisation layer of the university sphere was easily visible through the groups of Erasmus-students, who often spend time together at lunch tables while speaking loudly their native languages. The neighbour of my first flat in Oulu was an Erasmus-student from Spain and he occasionally invited me to gatherings. There were spoken many particular varieties of globalized English, and often these young people from different parts of Europe were exited about their experiences in Finland.

This young university, located about seven kilometres from the city centre, included many applied sciences establishing important bases for communication technology related to entrepreneurship in the Oulu region. The Department of Geography belongs to the Faculty of Natural Sciences (following the common German model of integrated earth sciences). Some academic traditions could be noticed implicitly. For example, the dimensions of sciences got hinted at every once in a while when crossing the geology stone-exposition on my way to the university office. Additionally, the walls of the department's corridors presented some three-dimensional models of physical landscapes and many maps with research results indicating particular patterns. The walls of the department coffee room presented portraits of the geography professors. The diversity of geography could be read from the professor's poster stands located usually beside their office doors. There appeared title pages of their published books or journals, a few travel photos beside the seminar, and lecture information. These corridor posters co-existed with research personnel pages on the Internet to describe their interests and achievements as well.

It was possible to witness some changes of the university work, which were encountered rather critically at Oulu University in the period of 2004–2007. One example of these changes can be the application of the result based salary system in the research work context. This meant additional bureaucracy even for young scholars to indicate their achievements and expectations. The pressure of publishing in high-ranked peer-reviewed journals increased. We chatted with colleagues and some sarcastic humour got articulated against the accelerated speed and rigid result measurement of academic research. However, people become more concerned about selecting the journals to publish in, about impact-indexes and about time frames of their dissertation projects. Result-oriented demands were extended to the departments as well. This is one reason why some geography departments at Finnish universities got conjoined with neighbouring disciplines.

Encounters at the University and Beyond

Usually dance is performed together with partner(s) and accompanying music. Similarly, the research is individual work involving colleagues and various situations of interaction. The research personnel (including PhD students) had their private office rooms. Thes small chambers provided quiet placse for reading, thinking, and writing. Most people kept their office doors closed and others half-opened. I tried both ways. It was rather annoying when one of the neighbours slammed his door very loudly. My office changed the location once after returning from the fieldwork, which lasted about a half year. The latter work-chamber happened to be on the second floor, the one of the professors, due to practical reasons. This was a new situation, which created some informal meetings and talks along the corridor.

The corridors of the Oulu university building(s) were very long. Some people used particular bicycles to move between the offices. The campus university contained several connected (mostly) one-floor buildings built in different periods. The passage from my office to the library took usually about five minutes and in winters it was needed to cross the rather cold glass-corridor between the buildings. The sharp colours were used to mark directions. This labyrinth type of building included several cafeterias. Often people checked the daily menu beforehand prior to choosing the lunch place. The state supported the meals of students, therefore the prices were reasonable. The university building was surrounded by trees and parking lots. The buses offered public transport connections to Oulu's town centre, and bicycles were widely used as well. Some tall dormitory buildings with nine floors stand just beside the university. A few shops and smaller student houses were located within a ten-minute walking distance. The campus and its surroundings were rather quiet and empty in the evenings. Similar tendencies of the campus university I encountered for example at the Ruhr-University of Bochum, Germany, where the electrical underground train links the campus with the urban centre.

The office hours at the Oulu university department were flexible. There didn't exist a particular card system to document the arriving and leaving at/from the building. Most of my colleagues followed the common 9-to-5 or even 8-to-4-o'clock rhythm at the office. Many people had families with children who required care after work. My weekly activities and concerns (particularly in first months) were much more related to the university compared with those of the colleagues who had lived in Oulu for longer. However, the beat of the university work extending over everyday life was quite much my own choice, not an externally forced one. The coffee meeting room provided a place for interaction in the department. Some people went there regularly around at 10 a.m. and at 3 p.m. to drink coffee and chat there. The cross-country skiing competitions of the Olympic Games were collectively watched and commented on as well. The lunchtime was important to talk with colleagues about research and everyday matters, although it was difficult to get used to the early lunch hours of Finns (11 a.m. onwards). The weekly rhythm of the department was organised every

Wednesday meeting. One member of the personnel (on the basis of a voluntary list) had to prepare coffee and bring cookies to the respective meeting. There were discussed institutional issues, experiences from the conferences and some university news. The relationships between the researchers were good; some tensions emerged between professors and younger researchers. This department had six professors of geography, thus there was a slight friction between these specialised fields as well.

Beside smaller groups there also existed collective initiatives, which aimed to include the whole department. For example, every spring, there was organised the trip-seminar to near-by sites of Oulu. The ice-ball trainings brought many colleagues together. I participated there a few times, although my skills in this fast game were limited. The small-Christmas and birthday parties were often continued in the city until the early morning only to grab some pizza before going home. Some pubs were more popular: "Never grow old" with simple furniture played interesting music, and "Kulma" (corner in Finnish) presented a fire show (with a *Rammstein* song) while ordering the signature cocktail. The restaurant "Uusi Seurahuone" close to the Oulu's market square provided a solid and celebrative atmosphere for the traditional dinner (*karonkka*) after my dissertation event.

The closest sphere of the communication was the research project community. We came together to discuss some thematic literature or just to have lunch in the cafeteria. Once or twice in the semester, there was organised a wider research project meeting, where researchers/PhD students talked about their achievements and plans related to the dissertation projects. The discussion language was usually Finnish. I tried to use Finnish as well, but sometimes switched to English to make myself more understandable. The switching between languages was a bit confusing and I missed some nuances of expressions. The non-Finns (we were two Estonians) researchers proceeded a bit slower in the first phase of the dissertation. A deeper knowledge about northern Finland and Scandinavia helped some researchers more easily to focus their interests in the project. The initial project group got partly widened in the middle phase when new PhD students also took part in the thematic discussions.

The periods of more intensive communication in the project team were shifted by the dispersed relations while doing field-work or visiting conferences. The face-to-face meetings created important situations alongside more loose ways of exchanging ideas over the Internet. This communication sphere enabled to present and negotiate the research plans and findings in the project group. According to Hautala (2011; referring also to Bart Nooteboom) group members with different cultural and professional backgrounds have different knowledge bases and therefore cognitive distances. But, too high a degree of cognitive proximity can reduce the possibilities to learn or create novel associations. It seems that in our research group there were encountered multiple frictions between cognitive proximity and distance for creating common understanding in knowledge creation.

My research grant provided finances for the period of 2004–2006. The contract was done for a year and then prolonged after discussing the research plan. The latter phase of the thesis after year 2006 got financed by smaller grants obtained from Finnish foundations and the Geography Department of Oulu, which were interested to support nearly ready dissertations. It means that the financing situation included uncertainties, although the first part of the research was well covered. The writing of applications became an essential part of doing research. The publishing of the dissertation papers took far longer time than expected. The post-doctoral initiatives were not particularly encouraged by the university services. The research group become more fragmented in a latter stage and there was certainly a lack of energy to look into a prospective post-doctoral period. This situation was partly triggered by emotional motivations to change my place of living towards southern Finland and Estonia. It means that cognitive frictions in the research group may include different matters and entangled negotiations.

Some research community members became my friends. This created an important communicative sphere, because I got to know few people from outside of Oulu University. Some colleagues invited me to their homes and introduced me to their family. These evenings with a good meal, wine and often sauna created nice atmosphere. The skiing trips and badminton trainings with the colleagues were also great alternatives to the university environment. I lived within walking distance from the university and often used bicycle as well. It was possible to rent the apartment through the student housing bureau. I considered several times to move to downtown Oulu. The bicycle roads of Oulu were in excellent condition in regard to the heavy snow falls. Many people use a bike all-year-around by wearing warm cloths and using special ice-tyres. I liked to take walks along the seashore wondering about white nights or too long winters. Sometimes I went skiing in the Kuivasjärvi area and enjoyed a tea with delicious *munkki* afterwards in a small cafeteria near the skiing tracks. For a certain period, I had even a car, which enabled me to visit some distant locations in northern Finland and Norway. There was quite much travelling to Germany and later to Helsinki to meet my girlfriend. The trip between Oulu and Helsinki took by train about six hours, although there was quite a good flight connection. It means that the travels from Oulu required efforts to visit family and friends. Sometimes I even became a bit nostalgic about life in Estonia. These entangled distances and efforts to overcome distances affected my private life, which was bound to the dissertation sphere as well.

Dispersed University Sphere and Revelations

The dancer can ignore some music beats and stress other varied rhythms through her movement. The doctoral system provides some basic tones that PhD students and (young) researchers can creatively fill with nuances and side paths or partly overdraw. This metaphoric expression describes some of the lines of doctoral studies in Finland. The dominating and often contested rhythms of the doctoral system can be described along the following (rather humble) pushes: the publishing in peer-reviewed journals, not to extend doctorate studies over four years, reporting about the state of dissertation project, and finding additional smaller grants. However, these pushes were balanced by several spheres in the dissertation process.

The doctorate students in Finland are clearly considered part of the main research staff. It means that PhD students have access to the wider research community and exchange of (tacit) knowledge. This creates an informal sphere with social rhythms that enable you to discuss and filter some of the above mentioned dominant (institutional) demands on dissertation projects. The young researcher as working part of wider projects has more possibilities for feedback. Here the horizontal initiatives appear very important. However, the communication between the young researchers and professors could in my case have been more regular and encouraging to avoid dropouts and extreme frustrations. The partial financing of the dissertation projects lowered thresholds to begin with research, although later, there may occur uncertainties. The common contract-based research salary covered the expenses well, and additional security can be provided by the trade union for academics. Some people still considered the dissertation in the Finnish system as a life-work (extending over a longer period of time) in regard to the wider generalisation and even devaluation of doctoral degrees on the job market.

If you compare the Finnish university tendencies and the position of doctorate students in the Estonian research system, the Estonian one is much more unsecure. This is influenced by the limited number of scholarships. Although in recent years there is introduced the status of 'young researcher' (with social security benefits) and the grant system encourages actively involving doctorate students. The research evaluation criteria in Estonia are highly dependent of peer-reviewed publications. The aim of foundations has been to create transparent and quantified database where research projects are described and the publications formally classified. This system tends to prefer logics of natural sciences and partly ignore some intrinsic characters of humanitarian and social sciences. The very recent reform of the Estonian grant system pushed to elaborate the wider platforms of research, and on the other side to create the intensive small research groups. The competition has increased, although some EU-funded programs provide additional options for international collaborations.

The push for interdisciplinary research becomes rather common. The unification of university departments or whole universities presents some of these tendencies. The academic disciplines have their traditions, concepts and methodologies creating particular approaches. My dissertation project was carried out at the geography department. The interdisciplinary dimension of the dissertation appeared mostly within the wide field of human geography. It means that many influences came from the social sciences, although the core group of collaboration were geographers. My recent research sphere at the Tallinn University was formally less structured according to the academic disciplines. Beside of interdisciplinary pushes there got formulated aims towards of trans-disciplinary research collaborations, which could create new knowledge beyond the single disciplines. The human geographers at Tallinn University (the traditional node of the academic geography education is still at the University of Tartu) were mostly bunched up at the research oriented Centre for Landscape and Culture as part of the Estonian Institute of Humanities. Social anthropology, semiotics, ethnology - these were some near collaborative disciplines for human geographers at Tallinn University. However, the challenges and lines towards transdisciplinary research are open.

The dance stage and dancers coexist with everyday life. Similar can be said about researchers and the related university spheres. Aspects of this emotional co-existence become visible with longer travels or change of living-place in abroad. There can be challenge to find good balance between work and leisure time of relaxing. The distance from previous everydayness may help to focus but are tiring in the longer run. Here appears the paradox that I have felt within the international university sphere to 'learn to sleep in the wind' (expression from Nigel Thrift) with simultaneously becoming identities and emotional belongings. This challenge can be encountered in multiple ways requiring efforts from mobile researchers and from university structures in Finland and elsewhere. The research group and the university departments are here a few 'bubbles' in the wider sphere of creative living. There can be built compact and well equipped university campuses (e.g. at Tallinn University) in urban areas, but vivid and novel knowledge achievements require additionally much more excessive characters.

The moments of surprise, insight, revelation, or sharp self-awareness – these compose experiences of flow which enable one to overcome alienation in everyday (Edensor 2010). These emotional components seem to be rather important for living and doing research work – wherever would it be culturally farther or closer areas. According to Csikszentmihalyi (1990) a 'flow' indicates an optimal experience in situations where attention can be freely pinpointed to fulfil own purposes. He adds that a flow requires the right balance between challenges and skills to realise the task. I would argue that this balance is important for inexperienced researchers to diminish fears and frustration of failure. However, a completely opposite situation with many skills and few challenges may generate boredom and the effect of "standing water" in the university sphere. Hautala (2011) argues that solutions to successful knowledge creation are not about how cognitively proximate or distant people are at a certain moment in time, but how they strive for cognitive friction. It means that international university spheres co-exist with multiple cognitive frictions. However, the challenge is to achieve dynamic 'bubbles' in the wider sphere, which enable creatively to rework frictions and generate flow-experiences in knowledge intensive work.

I would like to return to the metaphor of dance. The intensification of the presence in the international university research sphere becomes more visible through associated social rhythms and dispersed proximity dimensions. The lightness of slow foxtrot steps requires exercises. The multiple frictions get negotiated and redrawn along the dissertation project. The learning efforts usually do not appear clearly from published papers or short dance performance. Dance enables us discover and rework plural and performative skills, simulating both a greater sense of extant situations and a glimpse of new styles of (urban) living (Thrift 2008). Thus, there will remain chances of surprise and poetics of encounters within the extended university research sphere, which can be lived and proceeded along with multiple rhythms.

References

Csikszentmihalyi, M. (1990). *Flow: The Psychology of Optimal Experience*. Harper & Row: New York.
Edensor, T. (2010). 'Introduction: Thinking about Rhythm and Space', in Edensor, T. (ed.) *Geographies of Rhythm: Nature, Place, Mobilities and Bodies*, pp. 1–20. Ashgate: Farnhnam.
Florida, R. (2002). *The Rise of the Creative Class. And How It's Transforming Work, Leisure, Community and Everyday Life*. Basic Books: New York.
Hautala, H. (2011). Academic Knowledge Creation As a Spatio-Temporal Process: The Case of International Research Groups in Finland. *Acta Universitatis Ouluensis* A 584. University of Oulu.
Lefebvre, H. (2004/1992). *Rhythmanalysis: An Introduction to the Elements of Rhythm*. Continuum: New York.
Pikner, T. (2008). Evolving Cross-Border Urban Networks. Case Studies in the Baltic Sea area. *Nordia Geographical Publications* 37: 4. Oulu University Press.
Thrift, N. (2008). *Non-Representational Theory: Space, Politics, Affect*. Routledge: New York.

Acknowledgments

This research paper was supported by Estonian Research Council grant IUT3–2 and by the European Union through the European Regional Development Fund (Centre of Excellence CECT).

A PhD in Geoinformatics

Rangsima Sunila

Research work in Geostatiatical spatial modelling

I started my PhD studies in January 2003 and took two years maternity leave during the process so I completed the degree in 2009. It took me altogether five years to complete my doctoral degree. I studied at the Helsinki University of Technology (TKK in Finnish or HUT in English) at the Department of Surveying majoring in Geoinformatics. It has to be noted that the university was merged with other two universities, the Helsinki School of Business and Economics and the University of Art and Design Helsinki in January 2010, and it is now known as Aalto University. The topic of my research was spatial data modeling using Fuzzy and Geostatistical applications. The title of my dissertation was decided in the later years of my study by my professor. I worked closely with my supervisor and had many publications with her so it helped me to set the scope of my dissertation very well. At the time when I started the PhD studies in Finland, the programme did not have a time limit for degree completion unlike for example, in the U.S., so it did not impose pressure on PhD students. The PhD students had the freedom to plan their research and studies with the support from supervisors and professors. However, in the 2005 degree regulations, the Ministry of Education and Culture decided that the official graduation time for doctoral degree three to four years.

My research focused, as stated above, on the comparison of fuzzy and geostatistics application for spatial data modeling. I aimed to study the uncertainty and imprecision of geographical information in spatial data modeling. The spatial data model can be created with various Geographical Information System (GIS) applications. The comparison between these methods presents the advantages and disadvantages of each method and the difference of the results. The error margin from the fuzzy model is higher than the geostatistical model but on the other hand, the fuzzy model is less complicated in terms of model construction and computation. However, when high accuracy is required for the decision making, the geostatistical model is recommended. There are two main factors to consider how to select the suitable method for the modeling, which are expert knowledge and data sufficiency. The study also presented that the geostatistical model can be adjusted in order to increase the accuracy of the result by applying the expert knowledge into the model.

Research situation in Finland

The career at the university is also more open than earlier years, for example; there is a tenure track programme which gives opportunities for the graduated PhD students to build up their career in the academic field and the programme is open for international PhD graduated students as well. (http://www.aalto.fi/en/about/careers/tenure_track/, access date: 20.07.2013)

After graduation, I have continued working at the department as a visiting lecturer for Geostatistics course besides my main work in the education consulting company. It is common that after the doctoral degree completion, the graduated students leave the research group and start their careers somewhere else. But, there are PhDs who prefer to continue working in the academic field, and they can apply for postdoctoral positions. I got some information from my colleagues that there are GIS projects assigned for master and doctoral degree students so that they can use the knowledge and results from their publications, theses and dissertations. The work process is pretty much the same as the system before the change of the university structure. It has to be pointed out that there has been a big change in the department of surveying since I graduated in 2009. The department was restructured and its name was changed to the Department of Real Estate, Planning and Geoinformatics (Department of Real Estate, Planning and Geoinformatics, access date: 20.07.2013)

The research positions in the university in Finland are not permanent positions for example, at my university (HUT). It can be problematic for one who wants to settle down in Finland after graduation, especially for foreign students. The duration of the employment is based on the project duration. So, one may have to live without work for a couple of months while waiting for the project approval. In my opinion, to be able to find a job outside the universities in Finland, knowing the Finnish language is a major plus. Although there are careers that do not require the knowledge of Finnish, these fields are rather scarce in the work market.

However, in my case, the GIS research experience benefits me most particularly in Thailand. The skills and knowledge are needed in many areas, for example research units in the universities, projects with the government sectors, and business organizations. The GIS knowledge is relatively new, and there are not many experts in this field especially in geostatictics. Thus it is a very good opportunity for me to find a position and build up my career in Thailand.

Working relationship, financial situation and living conditions while working as a researcher

I have been working within the geoinformatic research community for almost ten years. I started as a research assistant, and after one year I became a researcher. Then, I was a teaching assistant and presently I am a visiting lecturer. I have very good relationships at work, and all of my colleagues are very nice and helpful. Whenever I encounter big or small problems, I always find help and support, especially from my professor and colleagues. Our research group is multicultural and international. The cultural differences are not the problem at all, which creates a nice atmosphere at the workplace. I really appreciate working with this research group because everybody is willing to share their knowledge and support each other when needed. Some of my colleagues became my close friends. And, we still keep in touch even they do not reside in Finland any longer.

The first winter in Finland was very long, cold and depressing for me. I come from a country where the weather is always warm or hot, i.e. Thailand. I lived in Australia before I moved to Finland, but the winter there cannot be compared to the Finnish winter. In Australia, snow can be found only in the mountain areas. The normal temperature in winter there is the same as during the spring in Finland. During that time, I got a lot of support from my colleagues who taught me to enjoy winter activities and white snow. I was very thankful for this.

Unlike in Thailand, the hierarchy in the organization in Finland is flat so that the relationship between the professors and students is not very formal. In Asia, the PhD students do keep distance with the professors and the title is always used whilst addressing one's superiors within professional hierarchies. In Finland, the students are treated equally and can call the professor by their first name without his/her title. The students can argue, discuss and disagree with the professors in the classroom. In Asia, the disagreement should be discussed at the professor's office or outside the classroom. The positional gap between the professors and PhD students in Finland is quite narrow, and it creates comfortable relationships. I felt very comfortable to discuss the problems of my research and ask for help from my instructor and professor without hesitation.

The salary from the project work and laboratory was the main source of income I got while I was studying towards my PhD in Finland. In my opinion, it was sufficient for a single student. In addition, there are many scholarships and stipends that PhD students can apply for. I got a scholarship from TEKES, The Finnish Funding Agency for Technology and Innovation, when I started the research in the first year. So, apart from the salary I got from the project, I got a scholarship to support my study in the first year which was very good in a way that I spent it on books, materials and IT equipment. My first research work was funded partly by the Geological Survey of Finland for a one-year term of contract. The topic of the research was using fuzzy application to model imprecision soil polygon boundaries. During the second year, my research was funded by the laboratory because I got a position at the laboratory as a researcher and teaching assistant. So, I was employed while I was doing the PhD coursework and dissertation. Although the position was not permanent, but merely a three-year term, it gave me enough time to complete my doctoral degree. Nowadays, there are many scholarships for foreign students to study towards master's and doctoral degrees in Finland, e.g. ERASMUS and CIMO.

I may say that being employed and working at the university while studying is a very good experience. In my country, students do not need to earn while studying. Their parents take care of the tuition fees and all other expenses until graduation. I learned a lot while I was working and studying at the same time. I learned how to manage my time effectively to balance study and research time. I learned to be responsible for the course I was assigned to give, e.g. a lecture or exercise. I gained experience in working at the academic institute. I had opportunities to participate in several conferences and seminars. I had the chance to learn other things outside the topic of my research from colleagues from many countries. All of these experiences are invaluable.

I knew many foreign PhD students while I was studying at TKK, and most of them were employed by the departments or laboratories, so they did not have financial problems. Their salaries were provided through research projects. However, sometimes, the project was discontinued and it caused lacks of funding for some time. From my experience, the university had its own scholarships to support PhD students in these cases. Many foreign PhD students I knew got the scholarships from the countries where they were from, and they were aware about the minimum financial requirement per month to live in Finland as stated in the visa application rules. So, for those students, especially students from Asia, the financial problems were not an issue unless they could not graduate within the time limit, usually four or five years depending on the field of study. After the graduation, a postdoctoral position is an option if one would like to continue working in the research field. However, there are not many postdoctoral positions open each year. The nearly graduated PhD students are recommended to seek positions before the degree completion, especially foreign students. Usually, the foreign students who get scholarships from the institutes in their countries have positions already pending after graduation. Besides, the doctoral degree does not guarantee a higher income after graduation. Some of my friends earn less than when they were researchers in the Finnish universities, even though they work in Finland. Of course, the salary also depends on the job description and responsibilities.

Finnish research and teaching experience

The research work in Finland gave me a splendid experience. I had little experience in research work before I came to Finland. At the laboratory of geoinformatics, I learned how to conduct research and write publications. The research in Finland is supportive. For instance, in the first year of my PhD study, my professor assigned me in the project to study the uncertainty in geographical information systems. I was guided to study new knowledge, fuzzy and geostatistical theories. At that time, I was not familiar with all the fuzzy concepts in which membership functions were used instead of crisp or non-crisp concepts. During the research, the fuzzy concepts and theories course was arranged in Helsinki, and there also was a conference organized in Estonia. I had a great opportunity to meet professor Zadeh, the main expert on fuzzy theories, and study the fuzzy theories under his guidance. I used the knowledge from that course to solve the problems in my research, and subsequently had three publications from the project. I do not have research experience in other countries than Finland but based on the information from friends, doing research in Finland is very supportive. The PhD students are encouraged to learn new theories and methods all the time. When new theories emerge or knowledge is required, laboratories or departments provide support to obtain that knowledge, for example by inviting the expert or professor from overseas to give lectures on the subject or sending the PhD students to attend seminars or conferences to exchange and gather the relevant knowledge. The expenses are taken care of by the laboratory or through the project's funding pool.

I started with the research assistant position in the first year of my PhD study. The main focus was learning how to conduct the research. I learned how to collect the data for the research, gather expert knowledge, apply the theories, process the information and write the papers. At the same time, I had to complete the coursework. The doctoral degree programme comprised coursework as well as thesis work. The study plan comprised the scientific practices and principles, theoretical studies and the research field. The study plan was discussed and agreed upon mutually with the supervising professor. In the second year of my studies, I got a researcher position and I started to assist the lecturer in the part of course's exercise. I learned the teaching skills through being an assistant in the course. In the later years, I was assigned to be one of the lecturers in the course, in which my colleague and I taught the course together. Subsequently, I got an assistant position, which was on a three-year contract. Close to graduation, I became responsible for Principles of Geostatistics Course.

The teaching community at TKK is helpful and supportive. I could ask for help from my colleagues anytime I needed it. When I started to plan my lectures in geostatistics, my professor gave advice how to plan the single lectures, build up the course structure and do the assessments. I also got support from my instructor, who provided some materials for the course. To become a lecturer at the university, teaching practice and experience are important. I was not confident in teaching at the beginning, but nowadays I feel comfortable with it. From my experience, it started with the course observation. I observed the course that I was assigned to assist in the part of the exercise. The lecturer gave me tasks and instructions. I performed the exercise together with another colleague. The responsible lecturer was in the classroom as well if needed. Next, I was assigned to the course, in which I joined into give the lectures together with another colleague. The experience in handling the exercise lesson helped me a lot to make me feel confident in giving the lecture. I had to prepare the materials for the lecture by myself with the support from my colleague who had more experience in teaching. Then, the geostatistics course was assigned to me after I had had a couple of years of experience in the subject and the geostatistical application was chosen to be the topic of my PhD research. With the advice from my professor, instructor and experts, I could plan the course and set the course structure effectively. After several years of working as a lecturer, I may say that my teaching skills are quite strong, which I am very thankful for to my professor, who gave me the opportunity to practice these teaching skills. It is not so common in Thailand that PhD students are assigned to teach while they are studying for their doctoral degrees. Many fresh PhDs face this problem when they start to work as lecturers because they do not have prior teaching experience. The teaching skill benefits me when I seek for a lecturer position in Thailand as I have both educational qualification and teaching experience. In addition, the doctoral degrees from overseas are more than welcomed in Thailand.

Research and teaching environment in Finland and Thailand

The research environment in Finland is very supportive in terms of funding, research materials, and equipment. There are a number of state and private organizations that support the funding for the research projects run through the universities. The budget for each research project is adequate and reasonable in order to cover the wages and expenses. I got information from my friends who were researchers in Thailand that the budgets for the research projects in Thai universities were quite limited, sometimes not even sufficient. This issue may bring about an uneasy research environment especially in the research field in which the specific equipment is required. As it was mentioned earlier, the organizational hierarchy in Finland is quite flat, and this applies also to the university organization. The gap between the supervisor and researchers is narrow, so this creates a relaxed and less stressful work environment. The working hours in Finland are reasonable, about 7.5 hours per day. Working as a researcher does not imply having a strict daily work schedule, and the research work can be done also outside the laboratory for example, one can write the research paper at home or in the library. In Thailand, the organizational hierarchy is quite strict, and there is a notable distance between the supervisor and researchers. The research environment in Thailand is quite formal and strictly rule-based. The working hours are about 8 hours per day, but usually researchers have long hours at work meaning that they usually stay in longer and without extra pay. It is common that researchers feel uncomfortable leaving the workplace before the supervisor. From my point of view, the research work environment in Finland gives researchers the freedom in work and deciding on their own work schedules. The supervisors do not interfere with the working time management of researchers. Of course, sometimes, it can be a disadvantage when one may lack motivation. The supervisor is more concerned about the results and outcomes of the research. On the other hand, the research environment in Thailand can be stressful, but may be the desired one for somebody who needs the control and readymade plans. There the supervisor can fully control a whole research project management plan to achieve the expected outcome.

I have experience in working in the education system in Finland for almost ten years. The Finnish education system is one of the best education systems in the world – judging from the PISA score. Why is the Finnish doctoral system successful? First, I would like to start with the point of view from lecturer toward students. In my opinion, I believe that it begins with the educational foundation. It begins with the primary educational system. The Finnish children are encouraged to explore knowledge and find solutions once they start kindergarten. The analysis and research skills are built up naturally. They learn to be innovative. They learn how to analyze and apply the knowledge to solve the problem. When they enter the university level, the analytical and problem solving skills are already strong. Within this topic, I would like to focus on the comparison between Finland and Thailand. The characters of Finnish students and Thai students are quite different. In Thailand, the students are told what to do. They learn to repeat and follow what the teachers provide them with. They do not often think creatively – in most cases. They learn to memorize the theories and methods. Although this should not be generalized too much, some Thai students are very good at finding solutions and have strong problem solving skills.

This is also supported by my observation through my class: the Finnish students have strong analytical skills, whereas Asian students are good at memorizing. The Asian students remember the theories very well, but they may be weak when asked to solve analytical questions. They are afraid that the answer may be wrong. The Finnish students have the courage to present their ideas no matter whether they are right or wrong. In the classroom, the Thai classroom is very formal. The students do not interrupt the lecture. If they have questions, they may ask the lecturer after the class end or visit his/her office later. The lecturer is addressed using his/her full academic title or position. In the Finnish classroom, the atmosphere is more relaxed and informal. The students are free to discuss and interrupt when they have questions. The lecturers are called by their first names. The aim of study for Finnish students is to learn, whereas Thai students have the goal to achieve excellent results in terms of high grades. I notice that sometimes those students who have high results cannot apply the theories to find the solution. The Finnish students care less about the grade but they are concern about what benefits they will get from the course.

The feedback from students came after the course end. I used that information to adjust the course contents and schedule for the next session. Sometimes, the contents were too much to fit in one lecture or too much work for assignments or the test was too difficult. It is two-way communication between the lecturer and students to achieve the objectives of the course with quality learning. One thing I learned from being a lecturer in Finland is trust. The supervisor who assigned the tasks to lecturers trusts the lecturers to be able to manage the courses. The lecturers trust themselves that they can do the teaching job effectively. The students trust that that they will be provided the knowledge from the professional. The whole process creates the aforementioned nice teaching and learning environment between instructors and learners. In Thailand, when the courses are assigned to lecturers, they are pretty much on their own to prepare and plan the courses. The learning and teaching environment is very formal. The students do not normally give feedback or comments after the course. The communication between instructor and students is one-way. In this case, the assessment is done by the supervisor, and the students' opinions may not be noticed.

Judging the Finnish doctoral system

I do appreciate the education system in Finland. The best thing about the Finnish education system is that everyone has equal opportunity to study, and that the education is free. It is similar to or the same as in other Nordic and many continental European countries. It also appeals to international students. However, there have been some changes. Currently, some universities and faculties start to collect tuition fees from non-EU international students, but the fees are affordable. This factor provides the country with high educated people and helps the country develop strongly. I appreciate that the doctoral degree study is not available only to ones who can afford the fees, but that it is rather open to anyone interested in his/her research field and would like to get an academic career started. So, in Finland, anyone can get the doctoral degree if they want to. Besides the non-paid doctoral degree education, international students commonly get financial support from their departments. The funding can be provided through the project work, scholarships and positions in the universities. Most of the scholarships do not required the students to pay the grants back to the supporters. In Thailand, the education is not free, and good education comes at a high price, particularly when doctoral programmes are concerned. It is a pity that the opportunity of getting an education is not for everyone. The PhD students in Thailand are mostly from those families who can afford the high tuition fees, or the students who get scholarships. The students who get scholarships are mostly entitled to work for the organizations that support the funding after graduation. The work contract can be up to ten years.

Finland is beautiful country with a clean nature and environment. The country is very safe, and things are run systematically. It is quite easy to learn to fit in the everyday life system. Studying in Finland gave me the opportunity to explore Europe. I had the chance to visit many countries, and many of those trips were through conferences. I had great opportunities to meet many professionals and experts. I had connections through my research and study.

The very important thing that I learned from PhD studies is the process of combining one's thinking, problem solving and analyzing skills. I learned how to analyze the problem given and find the solution by doing the relevant research. I have been in Finland for almost eleven years and I never have regretted my decision to come here.

A Doctorate in Germanic Philology in Finland – Process, Challenges, Perspectives

Michael Szurawitzki

Introduction

I received my doctoral degree from Åbo Akademi University[1], Finland's solely Swedish language university. The university offers a full range of courses and was founded in 1917, primarily to serve the needs of Finland's Swedish language minority, which today roughly represents six per cent of the country's population. Within many faculties, there are also courses offered in other languages than Swedish, which is the main language for both teaching and administration. Within the field of my doctoral studies, Germanic Philology, all teaching and research were/are carried out in German; only administrative tasks have to be carried out in Swedish. I am going to take a threefold approach in describing how my doctoral experience was like: Firstly, I am going to describe the process which led up to the completion of my doctoral thesis and its public defence and the later conferral of the degree. The second step will be to address challenges which had to be overcome whilst working on my manuscript, both in terms of content and logistics/administration. The third and last step will comprise thoughts on how the future of Germanic Philology in Finland might be like, both on the basis of what I experienced during my doctoral stage, and how it has evolved since then. Having spent many years within the Finnish university system, some matters – especially those of organization – might seem obvious to me, whereas others might not make too much of them. I will thus try to downshift from the outset, thus enabling any interested readership to follow my thoughts without any prerequisites in terms of expert knowledge. Subsequently, the first focus will be on the process of acquiring a doctorate in Germanic Philology.

Process

I received my doctorate in Germanic Philology from Åbo Akademi University on November 8th, 2005. My thesis was on the influence of Italian philosopher

---

1 www.abo.fi [3/5/2013].

Niccolò Machiavelli on English Renaissance (Christopher Marlowe's *Tamburlaine* and Shakespeare's *Henry V*) and German Baroque drama (Andreas Gryphius' *Leo Armenius*) (published as Szurawitzki 2005a). Machiavelli's main treatise on princely behaviour, *Il principe* (*The Prince*) of 1513, is read as a negative mirror-image of the ideal ruler as depicted in numerous medieval mirrors for princes, many of them from the German-speaking medieval world (which I analyze at length). It would be impossible to describe the results in only a sentence or two, a neat summary is offered in the printed version of my *lectio praecursoria*, the lecture I delivered as the inaugural part of my doctoral defence, which took place on September 23rd, 2005 (publication as Szurawitzki 2005b). I had graduated from the University of Turku little more than three years earlier (May 16th, 2002), having obtained my M.Phil. in English Philology with honours (a prerequisite to take up doctoral studies). The background in English literature explains the strong affinity to English philology as reflected in the comparative thesis I ended up writing and submitting in the field of Germanic Philology. I initially was admitted into Åbo Akademi University's doctoral program via the English Department in June 2002. A short e-mail inquiry and a brief interview combined with the distinction of my thesis (*magna cum laude*) sufficed to get me a doctoral position; in terms of official university administration. I had to come up with official record transcripts as well as a one-page research plan which had to be accepted by the Faculty of Arts (this procedure nowadays is taken care of by a special committee, no longer by the faculty). The downside of my admission to the English department's ranks was visible from the outset: there was no immediate funding offered. As a young researcher, I took it for granted that my supervisor did not sign any letters of support for the first six months. This should have set off an alarm bell. Some time later, I however managed to get a year-long research grant through the *department's* own research fund, something very rarely to be found within Finnish academia. The difficulties with my supervisor then became obvious also on a thematic level, since I did not manage to figure out in which direction my supervisor wanted me to work; I would retrospectively describe my year at the English department as not very giving. One fine day, I was suddenly and without any prior warning asked to step into my supervisor's office: either I was going to write an excellent essay of 50 pages on a certain subject within three weeks, or to leave the doctoral program. I had not seen this coming. Luckily, I intuitively did the right thing and walked up the stairs to the German Department, where I told my story to the Head of Department there. She thanked me for my open words, took a look at my work, read it overnight and the very next day came up with the necessary alteration steps to be taken to transform my work into a coherent doctoral thesis within Germanic Philology. Said and done: we drew up an alternative research plan, which passed the faculty, and I faced my old supervisor to officially resign from my post at the English department. Even though it felt difficult at the time, I still would call this a very smooth transition to the German Department, where I suddenly was to complete more required coursework in German (Germanic Philology had been my minor subject), but I had secured a new academic safe haven in literally no time.

The transition to the German department had taken place in October, 2003. From then on, everything went according to plan, and I was fortunate enough to enjoy the continuous attention of my supervisor, a medievalist who showed genuine interest in my research and who cannot be thanked enough. I made rapid progress and managed to secure new funding, now through the fund of Åbo Akademi University, making my life easier on the financial side. Thematically, I was able to advance very quickly, thanks to various archival research stays at Cambridge, Florence, and London (see also the *Challenges* part). I started delivering papers at conferences, thus accumulating the feedback necessary to make rapid progress. In the winter of 2004/2005, it came to finalizing the draft of my manuscript. It took me some more months to do so, but on March 7th, 2005, I submitted my 223-page manuscript, together with the necessary documentation, to Åbo Akademi University's Faculty of Humanities. Subsequently, two external evaluators were chosen to provide their feedback and to judge whether my work was of the necessary quality to be bound and printed as a doctoral dissertation. Some two months later the reports came in (one of them by fax!), and both were in favour of acceptance. I had simultaneously prepared my manuscript for publication, since in Finland, there is the practice of publishing the thesis *prior* to the public defence; this is a practice which is common to the Nordic countries, but which deviates strongly from many other countries, such as e.g. Germany. My thesis then was published with the academic publishing house Königshausen & Neumann in Würzburg, Germany, so that the public defence could go ahead in September 2005. In this respect it has to be mentioned that the publication of thesis prior to the defence is a mandatory step within the process of obtaining a doctorate.

In the public defence, I had to explain what I had done in my thesis in front of some fifty listeners and was examined by my official opponent, professor Dieter Heimböckel (now of Luxemburg University), for approximately 2 hours and 30 minutes. After that, the evaluation committee discussed my performance and came up with a grading proposal, which was later verified by the faculty council on November 8th, 2005. This is the date of my doctoral certificate as well. The certificate was handed to me without any noticeable ceremony some days later in the faculty offices; there was, however, a conferral ceremony called *promotion* on May 23, 2008, in which 112 doctors of Åbo Akademi University (including myself) ritually received their titles (again), now in a ceremony conducted in Latin during which the official insignia of a doctor were conferred (i.e. a sword, to represent the fierceness of the argument, a round doctoral cylinder hat, to represent the freedom of the argument, and a Latin language diploma stating that the conferral had taken place). This was a truly traditional end to a process that in practice had come to its close already three years earlier, i.e. when I had been issued with my doctoral certificate. When reflecting on this process now, close to eight years after its completion, it seems as though this was a highly swift procedure. This had to be explained against the background of my pursuit of a second degree after the doctorate, i.e. the so-called *Habilitation*. This official postdoctoral degree, which I obtained from Regensburg University in Germany in 2011, and which can be obtained from a number of European countries and certifies the formal professional qualification of the degree holder, took me roughly six years to finish; in comparison, the doctoral effort looks substantially smaller, and it also *is*. However, I felt proud as well as exhausted after having received my degree of *filosofie doktor*, to mention the official Swedish nomenclature. I have given a brief account of the circumstances in which my degree came about, without elaborating on the procedural challenges (apart from the change of supervisors, of course). In the following section, I will try and reflect different difficult situations I had to face, and how these difficulties were overcome.

Challenges

The challenges I had to face during my doctoral project were mostly of logistic and financial nature. As I have pointed out in the previous section, it was difficult to establish a financial basis to pursue full-time research. It was not a question of being admitted into a doctoral program that proved to be the main obstacle for me, as it might be for many others, who then are admitted with a four-year graduate school grant. Whereas I was admitted without difficulty or delay, I was faced with the monstrous task of finding funding, without the help of anyone (at least at the outset). Researchers in the Humanities in Finland generally face the difficulty of a severe lack of funding resources. There are both stately and private research funding organizations, funds (*säätiö* in Finnish) and graduate schools as well as doctoral positions directly advertised by universities. This seems like a complex and broad network at first glance, but proves literally impenetrable to the uninitiated in practice. Only at the end of my doctoral work had I gained a sufficient overview over the relevant and existent resources. In practice, one needs (or should need) the advice of a senior colleague on the professoral level willing to share the necessary amount of knowledge with you, otherwise an academic career can well be over before it really starts; I've witnessed various examples of ambitious projects collapsing either well before being finished, some close to the finish line; some people even get their doctoral degrees and want to continue as postdoctoral researchers, but run out of money at that (very tough) stage, and thus are forced to pursue a career outside of academia.

In my individual case, I could not rely on the generosity of a multi-year grant provided by a graduate school, which possibly could have proved the smoothest of options. I rather had to look and apply for six- to ten-month grants continuously, luckily for me with a fairly high rate of success. I do not want to imagine what would have happened if I had not managed apply for money as successfully as I ended up doing. The constant pressure I faced had different impacts: firstly, I was forced to be productive and to constantly drive my project forward. This led to more advanced and refined funding applications, which in turn mostly led to yet another grant which provided me with the necessary freedom to bring my doctoral project further towards a completed thesis. This was the positive impact my situation had on my work; however, quite obviously, there is also a flip side to this coin. The constant financial insecurity was, at times, something that was hard to bear. I shared this fate with quite many young colleagues; yet, a common situation like this one is not necessarily always perceived as 'common'. One tends to look for flaws in oneself, in the project etc., only to eventually discover that it actually is the system's flaw. The kind of academic Darwinism, which was prevalent in the circumstances I experienced and endured during my time as a doctoral student in Finland, is quite tough, to be frank. I am quite convinced that facing the amount of pressure that I just laid out cannot be everybody's cup of tea. There are, just like in any Darwinist approach, two ways which you can/will encounter: either success (most likely as the result of personal sacrifices) or failure, which in the case of doctoral studies most likely will mean dropping out without having any chance of completing the doctoral degree, ever. Those who manage to secure themselves a spot in the graduate schools that Finland has to offer since roughly 2000 to the present day (after 2015, all universities will have to have own graduate schools, the stately-run schools will be abolished), quite naturally, focusing on technical and natural sciences), probably even prior to moving to Finland, do not have – on the basis of what I've learnt from numerous conversations – the faintest idea of how lucky they *can* and *should* consider themselves (even though, as my formulation implies, most people do not; instead they complain about too little pay etc.).

Even though the funding of one's doctoral degree is one of the core issues that has to be given thought constantly, there are also other aspects that spring to mind, especially in my case, when reflecting the challenges I had to face and overcome in pursuit of the desired title of *doctor philosophiae*. My subject was quite complex, combining the expertise of a number of subjects such as English and German literature, medieval studies, Early Modern history, philosophy and political thought, Renaissance studies and comparative aspects as well as literary theory. This mix of areas of expertise produced a constant need to travel abroad, since the Finnish libraries and their holdings often enough proved to be lacking core texts. Securing travel funding, on the other hand (against the background of the difficulties to get research grants), seemed relatively easy, since I managed to have the costs for all my trips to Cambridge, Florence, Oxford, and the British Library (the latter being explicitly well-stocked also in regard to Germanic literature of relevance to me, which in turn saved me further trips to Germany), as well as to my old academic homebase, the Ruhr-Universität Bochum, covered through the generosity of the fund of the Research Institute associated with Åbo Akademi University. In this respect I at times even found Åbo Akademi University quite generous and was puzzled what kind of stark contrast this marked against the sketched background of how difficult it actually was to get research grants. The generosity went further to the financing of conference travel to talk about my doctoral project, which included a trip to the Canadian Comparative Literature Association's meeting at Winnipeg in 2004, my first ever academic conference presentation. Travelling to archives was not as convenient in 2004 as it is today, since there were no book scanners at the time to digitize your material on the go. Moreover, I had to make the effort of a) taking lots of notes (mostly with pencil, since the restrictions were quite severe in most libraries, and power sources for laptops were relatively rare, compared to today; I won't mention the absence of Wi-Fi hotspots, which we take for granted today; no *Google Book Search* etc.), b) taking even more photocopies, or c) read Early Modern books in the restricted access reading rooms of Oxford and Cambridge as well as the Biblioteca Nazionale in Florence. Not every aspect of these experiences seems tough from my perspective today, but it sure felt tough whilst being in the middle of it. The digitization of lots of materials related to academic research of any kind must have cut down the amount of archival travel among researchers worldwide. Those who, like me, have had the pleasure or, I should say, the honour of working in archives closed to 'ordinary human beings', must be looking back on these times with ambivalent feelings. Of course it is convenient to merely download your material, but looking it up or discovering it in an archive or library is just something that is way more rewarding for you as someone loving what you do (i.e. research) than finding it through the oracles of the Internet age, i.e. search engine, which literally anybody literate can use. The digitization somewhat has deprived us researchers of some of the fascinating investigative 'detective-like' work which accounts for some fascinating aspects of our job. Luckily enough, during my doctoral studies, I was provided the infrastructure to follow through with this work and to successfully bring it to its conclusion.

Perspectives

Some of the aspects I am going to discuss under the heading 'perspectives' could also have fit into the 'challenges' section. I tried to mainly keep the 'challenges' part focused on my personal experiences during the doctorate's various stages. Now, however, is the moment to try and fit these into a bigger picture. The research infrastructure in the arts and humanities in Finland is too vast and subject-specifically differentiated to make generalizations of a broad kind realistic or even possible to utter. This is why I am going to stick to the situation of Germanic Philology, i.e. Germanic linguistics and literature, the subject area that I come from and that I know best when it comes to assessing the Finnish situation.

My experiences uttered above should and cannot be taken as a general example. From my point of view, every researcher is 'own their own' once they start their doctoral research. There is one of the safe havens I referred to, i.e. a graduate school, for language studies, which is called *Langnet*[2], with which I nowadays cooperate as a supervisor within the field of Applied Linguistics and act as referee for doctoral proposals. This graduate school unites the linguistic doctoral students of all modern languages departments in Finland; this makes the competitions for the advertised doctoral fully-funded positions tough. My view of this organization is ambivalent: on the one hand, it is convenient to offer a full graduate school to doctoral students of linguistics, on the other hand it seems that many of those accepted sit back and relax after having been admitted. Over the years, I have seen a number of examples of doctoral students from Langnet who simply either did not graduate or, to put it euphemistically, 'took their time', sometimes as long as ten years altogether. Sometimes it is puzzling enough to witness how especially these persons never seem to run out of funding, partly obviously due to their good networks, definitely not through their academic achievements. In Finland, there recently has been a discussion of whether the university system produces a too large number of doctorates. When it comes to linguistics, one can concur with this position in the respect that those taking over five years to graduate should generally be singled out. Sometimes, there are obstacles, such

---

2   For more information, see their website: https://www.jyu.fi/hum/laitokset/kielet/tutkimus/langnet/en [3/6/2013].

as pregnancies or taking over lecturer posts, which justify a prolonged status as doctoral student, but generally there should be more time pressure on those working towards a doctorate. A time span of five years is more than enough for most fields, and after five years' work one generally would have o go back and check the work done at the outset of that period (in contrast to merely preparing it for publication), since it might very well be outdated by that point. I know cases of researchers in my field who have been 'busy' writing their PhD thesis for more than ten years running (!). It is quite obvious that, should they manage to conclude their project, which the results cannot be of utterly high relevance to the scientific community, since the project itself was designed more than ten years ago. The research questions relevant back then might have been answered, and seem much less important today. Completing a doctoral project over ten years' time entails a lot of remodelling and reworking and continuously 'going back and forth', both in one's thinking and one's manuscript. There is a severe danger of not following through coherently with one's project, and thus I see no real point in (steadily) supporting doctoral students who simply are not able to finish their projects in a reasonable amount of time.

Whilst Langnet also has its good points, i.e. uniting researchers with interests in linguistics from different subject areas within modern language studies, I have to also look at the situation of Germanic linguistics in Finland itself, without the backup of this state-run program. I will limit myself to Germanic linguistics, even if I have talked about 'Germanic philology' so far, even if my own doctorate does not have a linguistic focus. This has to do with the core areas of Germanic language research in Finland, which can clearly be identified as lying within linguistics and translatology. One could argue that this situation is fairly clear-cut and should enable the various universities to flawlessly pursue cooperation schemes. In theory, this would be possible; in practice, however, the situation is quite different: puzzlingly enough, there are very few common projects. It is rather so that every department nowadays faces a vast amount of pressure since the universities were remodelled in their organizational structure, now resembling business enterprises, or, in terms of their main task, 'degree factories'. They are paid for producing MA and doctoral degrees, and for these degrees only. There is no money set aside for BA degrees or the Finnish intermediate degree between MA and PhD, the licenciate or *lisensiaatti*. Each department has to provide a prognosis of their goals for the coming year, and if you do not meet your goals, your position will be weakened, possibly resulting in funding cuts or even closing down the department.

Against this background, it can be understood why there cannot be a lot of cooperation between the departments when it comes to degrees (with, hypothetically, commonly supervised doctoral students). Who is eventually going to get the money? This will be the university actually conferring the degree. Thus, on the basis of the current system, there in practice cannot be a common supervision of a doctoral student by two Finnish universities, since one university would have to voluntarily let go of a six-figure euro sum of *Mehrwert* (in Marx's words), whilst the other would get the sum in question and a PhD under its belt. This is a very strange situation, since the university departments in Finland (especially with reference to my field, i.e. Germanic linguistics) could strongly benefit from more mutual cooperation. The system, however, does not encourage such endeavours, to put it mildly.

The situation just sketched is fairly new to the Finnish academic environment; one must address the question whether the hesitation to cooperate thus is a new phenomenon as well. On the basis of Germanic linguistics and philology, my answer to this is a clear 'no'. The cooperation efforts could have been better before that as well. In times in which organizations tend to focus on big and powerful clusters, the departments in my field – generally speaking – operate more or less alone. I see this as highly dangerous, since being a small department makes it easier to be abolished. Of course, there are ties within the faculties of a single university (such as the Department of Modern Languages in the University of Helsinki[3]), but there are no official institutionalized cooperations between German departments (apart from very few projects), and this might prove fatal in the long run. University mergers have taken place already, the most prominent being Helsinki's Aalto University, which emerged through combining Helsinki's University of Technology, the Helsinki Business School, and the local University of Design (also the University of Eastern Finland is e.g. formed out of the Kuopio, Savonlinna, and Joensuu campuses[4]); there is, at least in my view, the need for department mergers as well. To give you a concrete example: the German departments of the University of Turku (comprising Germanic philology, translatology and interpreting) and Åbo Akademi University are situated roughly 500 metres from each other. Logistically and in terms of establishing a powerhouse of German research in Turku, this would make sense. Due to the differing organizations, however, this seems less than likely to happen in the near future, if ever. The need to join forces is stronger than at any point in the history of Finnish academia; the two departments mentioned could even stay in their respective buildings, one would have to have common leadership and administration 'only'; with the less clear-cut hierarchies in Finland this

---

3 http://www.helsinki.fi/modernlanguages/ [3/6/2013].
4 http://www.uef.fi [3/6/2013].

could be possibly established. I strongly doubt that there is the will from either side to pursue such a merging project; as long as an existence of its own can prevail, it also *will* prevail. At some point in time this might have proven fatal for some department; the future will tell.

One last point I would like to elaborate on within the auspices of this paper is the reciprocal impact the German departments (should) have on each other. Here it has to be mentioned that the spectrum of departments ranges from some universities with just one professor via universities with two professors to the University of Helsinki with three professors (even though these are broken up into two professorships of Germanic philology and one professorship of German translatology, respectively in two sub-departments of the aforementioned large Department of Modern Languages). The perspectives can, for the most part, be characterized in the way that the smaller departments look up towards their bigger counterparts with some envy. For the bigger departments, it does, when reversing the perspective, *not* necessarily mean that they are more secure in their existence. I do not see very much common effort between the single departments, even though there exists enough common ground. The most recent gathering I was able to participate in was the *Finnischer Germanistentag* held at the University of Helsinki in October, 2012. The panel discussions there could not show how there could be common efforts in the near future; the fact that conferences like these are held only every three years speaks for itself. In my view there is a lot of potential of developing the common ground, in terms of the subjects researched, as well as facing and eventually (hopefully) overcoming the constantly changing problem sphere of the implementation of the Finnish university reforms. Today, we cannot know for sure whether Germanic philology will exist in its present form in ten years' time; most likely, it will not, and only very few strong centres will have survived, Helsinki being one of them as the capital and as the strongest department of today. The strategic efforts of all other departments will determine their respective futures, since it will become inevitable to search for alternative 'forms of existence', for it is already difficult to secure constant funding. All in all, it has become simply a matter of money. There is no place for such things as tradition, trade relations (Finland-Germany), originality or quality of research any longer. The end of the *universitas* in the traditional sense is already dawning on Finland, since research foci are narrowed down under the dictate of global business questions. The immediate effect is a much more pragmatic orientation when it comes to pursuing a PhD in Finland, above all in a thematic sense. Funding questions thus also become relevant: if there is no concrete interest in your subject, securing the relevant financing can be extremely challenging.

References

Szurawitzki, M. (2005a): *Contra den rex iustus/rex iniquus? Der Einfluss von Niccolò Machiavellis Il principe auf Christopher Marlowes Tamburlaine, Shakespeares Heinrich V. und Andreas Gryphius' Leo Armenius*. Würzburg: Königshausen & Neumann. 218pp. (= *Epistemata Reihe Literaturwissenschaft* 550)

Szurawitzki, M. (2005b): Contra den *rex iustus/rex iniquus*? Der Einfluss von Niccolò Machiavellis *Il principe* auf Christopher Marlowes *Tamburlaine*, Shakespeares *Heinrich V.* und Andreas Gryphius' *Leo Armenius*. Lectio praecursoria. *Neuphilologische Mitteilungen* 106: 349–356.

A triangular PhD experience – Germany, Canada, Finland

Mischa Theis

A Few Words About Myself

When I was asked to contribute to this book, I already had been out of academica for seven years. Barely one month after my graduation during the beautiful summer of 2006, I disappeared into a big multinational company within the chemical industry and have not looked back ever since. So am I really a good judge to elaborate on the Finnish university system now, as it is an experience from a long-gone past? I believe that I am because my view is that of an outsider, and never having thought of pursuing a PhD when entering university in the first place, my account may give the reader a view that most likely differs from that of my fellow contributors who may be still pursuing an academic career.

While my memory may fail here and there, I have done my very best to give an analytical account of the four years that undoubtedly belong to the best ones of my life. However, this account being a personal reflection rather than a well-researched article, I apologize in advance for any inaccuracies that time may have inflicted upon my memory.

My way to Finland

From Germany...

How come I ended up in Finland, especially since I have no ties to this Nordic country at all? Well, it came like this: I am of German origin, born 1976, and decided to take up a Master degree's study (diploma) in Chemical Engineering in 1996 at University of Dortmund, which was sufficiently close to my home city of Cologne. During my studies I decided to spend a year abroad with the main intention to hone my English skills while expanding my horizon as well. My choice was Canada, as England looked too close to home (culturally still pretty European despite persistent claims to the contrary), while other Anglophone countries with strong technical background were either perceived unsafe for comfortable living (South Africa) or already quite well-known to me by that time (United States and Australia).

The successful application for a DAAD (German Academic Exchange Service) scholarship then cast the dice for University of Toronto, and I have never regretted my fate since. While spending a comfortable academic year 2000/2001 in Toronto, I took on a four-month research project at the Pulp and Paper Centre and got associated with its strong ties to research institutions around the world. A particularly strong tie based on several personal friendships existed with Åbo Akademi University in Turku, Finland. I started to hear good things about the Process Chemistry Centre over there.

... via Canada ...

When my exchange student year was drawing to a close, I was offered to return as a PhD student with the Pulp and Paper Centre once my Master degree had been completed in Germany. With only half a year to go in Germany and merely the diploma thesis missing, this was suddenly a realistic option to consider. Before this particular offer my mind was rather set on starting to work straight away in the chemical industry in the Cologne area, and if possible, then for the company for which I have been working ever since completing my PhD. At that time I was not quite looking at the academic value of the PhD student offer, but considered it rather as a suddenly-opening avenue for living just a bit longer in the city that I had begun to fall in love with: Toronto.

When discussing the details I remembered the strong ties to Åbo Akademi University and began toying the idea of having a joint project that could include several research stays in Finland, which at that time was to me still an obscure little country on the northern edge of Europe that was best reached from Canada via Frankfurt (offering convenient stopovers at home). While my lust for adventure was one part of the motivation, the opportunity to work together with not just one, but two professors who were considered absolutely top-notch in their field of research was the second part. We agreed in principle on the possibility of a joint research project, with details to be sorted out while I was completing my Master's degree back home in Germany. So far the mindset was to enroll for the PhD program at the University of Toronto with several research stints at Åbo Akademi University.

... to Finland

A first visit to Turku in the summer of 2001 gave me the impression of an empty place with a Soviet-inspired main square: not very appealing at first sight. But I also got the impression of visiting a highly sophisticated technical society, and I was particularly impressed by the well-equipped research centre at the Åbo Akademi

Process Chemistry Centre. Talking details on possible research topics and feasible project setups then tipped the scale towards Åbo Akademi as my *alma mater* and Toronto as the destination for several research stays: no hassles with immigration, no issues with administration, no need for the translation of any documents, full recognition of the German Master's degree and, on top of that, roughly double pay (after taxes) for the same work.

A conference call a short time later between Turku, Toronto and Cologne then fixed the matter, and the research topic was set up in general with details still to be settled later. It was as easy as that. In summary, what brought me up to Finland? A lot of random events for sure, but once the opportunity arose, it was a mixture of Finnish pragmatism, determination and excellence in research that persuaded me to give it a try.

My PhD Experience

The Research Topic

I started in March 2002 as a research associate at the Laboratory for Inorganic Chemistry at the Process Chemistry Centre of Åbo Akademi University. We decided to settle on the topic of "Interaction of Biomass Fly Ashes with Different Fouling Tendencies", as biomass like bark is an important byproduct of the pulp and paper industry, and biomass as such is also fired widely together with coal or peat in many Nordic power boilers with the purpose of generating electricity. Hence we would have an elegant combination of topics relevant both to Canada and Finland.

The rationale behind the research was that the ash of biomass has quite low melting points and tends to stick to the walls of the boilers, while the ash of coal and peat melts at comparatively higher temperatures and is less sticky. The PhD thesis had the goal to investigate what happens to the stickiness of the ash when different types of biomass and coal or peat are fired together and to arrive at explanations of the observations.

The arrangement was such that all preparation work and post-experimental analyses were carried out in Turku, while the experiments were performed in a large furnace (simulating actual boiler conditions) that was located at the Pulp and Paper Centre in Toronto. The experiments were carried out over a time period of 1.5 years altogether, while individual stays in Toronto ranged from two to six months.

Funding

Funding was received during the entire period from Åbo Akademi University in form of a regular salary as per four-year contract. The contract started as a one year contract that was extended in due time in a manner similar to the probationary period in industrial life. Additional expenses for living in Toronto, such as furnishing a room and renting with friends, were covered on top of the regular salary.

My research work at the Åbo Akademi Process Chemistry Centre as a national Centre of Excellence was funded through three pillars: a "local pillar" in form of Åbo Akademi University itself, a "national pillar" in form of TEKES (The National Academy of Technology of Finland), and an "industrial pillar" in form of a research consortium consisting of six multinational companies in the paper and boiler businesses.

The "local pillar" was made more effective by combining forces with three other laboratories inside of Åbo Akademi's Chemical Engineering department (creating the Process Chemistry Centre) as well as clustering with three more technical universities in Finland (Helsinki, Lappeenranta and Oulu). The "national pillar" was topped up by the award of the title of a national "Center of Excellence" to the Åbo Akademi Process Chemistry Centre. The funding through the industry was obtained in a form of a regular member fee, which bears the advantage to the member companies to obtain a wide range of research results for a very limited individual contribution.

Complicated as it sounds, as far as funding itself was concerned, my only direct involvement in the entire progress was active participation in the bi-annual consortium project review meetings as well as an application and subsequent reporting to the Graduate School of Chemical Engineering which is the organizational body behind the clustering of the respective PhD programs of Åbo Akademi University, the Helsinki University of Technology, Lappeenranta University of Technology and Oulu University. All fundraising, handling of grant applications and reporting was performed by senior staff, which meant that I was able to fully focus on the work that was required to obtain the PhD degree.

The PhD Program

A Finish technical PhD program usually consists of the publication of four to six papers in peer-reviewed journals as well the accumulation of 40 credits (equivalent to 60 ECTS credits), which amounts to the successful participation in about 13 one- to two-week courses. The PhD thesis as such is then a relatively short summary of the previously published papers as well as a discussion in the entire context that is then to be defended against an opponent from an external university.

The Courses

While the 13-odd courses to be selected should have reference to the area of research in form of a main and supplementary subject, there is still ample choice in picking individual courses themselves that can be tailored to personal interest. However, being a country of small population, filling these post-graduate courses at individual universities can prove a challenge. This observation may have been a contributing factor when setting up the Graduate School in Chemical Engineering and thus to join forces and offer joint courses.

In addition to the Graduate School in Chemical Engineering, similar such arrangements exist throughout the Nordic countries, combining various technical departments of Universities in Norway, Sweden, Denmark and Finland at national and pan-Nordic levels (possibly by now also more or less officially extended to the Baltic States). This approach not only widens the range of courses offered, but it also intensifies the scientific exchange of people and ideas. In my particular case, the cooperation of the Graduate School in Chemical Engineering with its Nordic sisters provided me with the opportunity to attend courses in interesting places such as Copenhagen, Stockholm and Gothenburg in addition to the "homebase universities" of Helsinki, Lappeenranta and Oulu.

My special arrangement with the frequent research stays at the University of Toronto also offered me an opportunity to attend courses over there. The huge flexibility of Finnish university administration enabled me to not only get credit for courses attended while not even technically being enrolled at University of Toronto, but also for courses taken during my past exchange student year as these courses have never been credited for the Master's degree. Here we come back to Finnish pragmatism that was a large deciding factor in joining for a PhD program at Åbo Akademi University.

Apart from these two sources for courses, I was also fortunate to be able to attend external courses in Essen (Germany) and Orlando (Florida). The course in Essen focused on operation of power boilers and was organized by the VGB (Verband der Großkraftwerksbetreiber). This offered me another good opportunity to look outside of the university environment and get into touch with industrial reality. The course in Florida was a plenary course on paper chemicals recovery boilers that happened to be hosted by my two supervisors and was tailored to an industrial audience in the Pulp and Paper business. Again, this was a great opportunity to expand my horizon beyond the ivory towers of my universities and get in touch with reality.

The Papers

Writing my research papers was clearly the most frustrating part of the PhD experience. Not only are papers slow to come by, but also they bear a high potential for frustrations caused by initial rejections by peer reviewers. The experimental nature of many technical PhD works explains the slow progress in producing papers: Experiments have to be well thought-out, loads of preparations and testing are to be done, a mass of data is accumulated that needs to be analyzed before any conclusions can be drawn. So one would expect an exponential increase in paper output: barely anything in the first years and all piling up at the end.

The rejections are part of the game. Nothing is more central to earning a PhD degree than gaining the ability to compile complex matters into a very limited space and still deliver the message. Popular belief has it also that another central part of a PhD degree is to stubbornly deal with a high degree of frustration and still not lose sight of the larger goal ahead. But this is only anecdotal evidence or plain gut feeling.

Four of my six papers were published in the *Fuel* magazine, while the remaining two consisted of conference proceedings in two separate issues of the *International Conference on Fluidized Bed Combustion*. As might be expected, the first paper in the *Fuel* magazine was the hardest to come by and needed the most revisions, both internally and after submission. However, once the right balance between necessary detail and required conciseness was found, the forthcoming papers have been much faster to come by. It also helped that different subsections of the same work were chosen for publication in separate articles, so that the writing was more or less overlapping, thus greatly speeding up progress.

The Posters and Conferences

The nicer part of the PhD work consisted of participation in national and international conferences where I had a chance to present my work to an audience of mixed background that included both academia and industry. This not only provided me with a good opportunity of networking, but it also increased my soft skills by honing presenting and defending skills. The conferences that I was able to participate in included not only the regular internal research consortia review meetings (annually in Toronto, bi-annually in Turku), the annual Process Chemistry Centre proceedings or the Graduate School reportings, but also the *Swedish-Finish Flame Days* (once in Vaasa, once in Gothenbug) and the *International Conference on Fluidized Bed Combustion* (once in Toronto, once in Vienna).

The two conference proceedings that found their way into my PhD thesis came from the two Fluidized Bed Conferences in Toronto and Vienna. The conference proceedings were a quite different kind of work compared to the papers that were published in the peer-reviewed *Fuel* magazine. In the conference proceedings, the main task consisted of condensing parts of the research topic into separate A0 posters with a clear graphical presentation concept. Writing up the more elaborate details behind the graphics was merely a few days' job in comparison.

Soft Skills

I had the very good fortune to have had two supervisors who interpreted their role to go far beyond my acquiring of mere academic skills. In partly attending the University of Toronto I had even more of good fortune to have the Dean of the Chemical Engineering department to be a close friend of both my supervisors and share their views on what would make a more complete education. This attitude allowed me to participate in several courses on improving scientific writing skills that were intended for native English speakers, never mind my distinct German accent. Not only was the writing style itself central to the course, but also the arranging of scientific evidence, its presentation and subsequent defending.

A very interesting feature of the Pulp and Paper Centre standard student education is the participation in an annual "Technology Tour". Alternating, this is either a "local" tour or an "international tour". The local tour usually consists of a week in the "close" vicinity of Ontario or Quebec, while the international tour is an approximately two-week long tour to a country with a strong background in pulp and paper technology. Countries visited in the past include the United States, Sweden/Finland, Japan, Brazil, or China. The technology tour comprises of visits to various research institutions as well as different industrial outlets ranging from the obvious paper mills to key suppliers of pulp and paper manufacturing technology/equipment. The main feature of the tour is that it is entirely organized by the students themselves (usually a group of 10–15), including the fundraising, although a contribution of 500 $ Cdn per student is made by the Pulp and Paper Centre for the international tours.

I was fortunate to participate in the 2004 international tour that had the destination of Brazil, as well as in the 2005 local tour that had the destination of Ottawa. As concerns the Brazil tour, after arriving in Sao Paulo for acclimatizing, we continued to Curitiba to visit a key supplier of paper machines before we set off to Belo Horizonte to visit the Pulp and Paper Department of the local university. The tour continued with a visit to Aracruz in Vitoria, then the world's largest pulp mill by output, before finishing off in *Ciudade Maravelhosa* (Rio de Janeiro) for purely touristic reasons. Being in an academic work environment then, I had no problems in continuing the touristic trip for another two weeks visiting Manaus, Belem and Fortaleza, thus giving me a more complete view of Brazilian culture. As concerns the Ottawa tour in 2005, apart from visiting local Carleton University, the obvious highlight was our stay with the research facilities of Atomic Energy of Canada where a surprisingly large lot of University of Toronto chemical engineers ends up being employed.

The Thesis

On all accounts that was the hardest part of the entire exercise. After returning from a September "ruska" holiday in Northern Lapland in September 2005, I set off to start writing the thesis at my kitchen table and initially estimated the exercise to be over in a month or two. After all, the required data were already neatly analyzed and presented in various papers, and all that was left to do was to summarize these papers and put them into a full context. Well, not quite so. Suddenly the deadline set for defense in June in order to be home for the 2006 World Cup in Germany became pressing, since this meant the final version had to be submitted no later than end of February.

This collided with another equally or potentially more important deadline: February is Carnival time in Cologne, and I had to be there even more than I had to be at home for the football World Cup. It ended in a classical *déjà vu* with Carnival exchanged for Christmas and PhD thesis exchanged for Master's thesis: Final printout at 4 am on the very last day and a hurried leave to Helsinki to catch a 10 am flight to Cologne...

The Defense

Finnish PhD regulations have it that the thesis is to be reviewed by an external auditor who will act as an "opponent" during the public defense of the thesis. "Public" means that all of the direct colleagues, anyone else from university interested in the topic, the industrial partners as well as friends and family caring and finding time will be present. This makes up quite some audience. After a short *lectio praecursoria* of approx. 30 min that is given by the defendant as an introduction to the topic, the opponent takes over and asks whatever question on the thesis came into his mind during the review of the thesis. It may not even be direct results of the thesis only, but also topics of general interest of the opponent's own research where he just searches a second opinion, as I later found out. This at times unpleasant interrogation exercise (modeled on the Spanish inquisition?) usually lasts for 2–4 hours, mainly depending on the mood of the opponent. In theory, anyone else from the audience holding a PhD degree may ask further questions, but my experience is that this rarely happens, as everyone is rather tired after the defence and is rather looking forward to cake and champagne.

In my specific case the opponent was from my native country and a professor at the Technical University of Munich. As hinted above, at times it got quite tough during the defense and my only solace was that I knew of his return flight at 5 pm, which meant that the nagging could not drag on eternally after the start at just 11 am. Unfortunately Turku Airport is very small and efficiently organized, which explains my all-time record of leaving the city centre on one occasion a mere 45 min before my flight was due to be leaving. I think my opponent came quite close to this record, but at least we found some time to have one toast of champagne. To neatly summarize this exercise, I'd like to quote one "non-scientific" sailor friend of mine who gave me good marks on what he called a pretty good swimming exercise. Maybe the barbecue under the midnight sun on the shores of the Baltic Sea the evening before (including German sausages and a 10 litre keg of Cologne beer) together with my family and a few friends was not as smart an idea for relaxing the mind as it seemed at that time.

Comparison Finland – Canada

The differences between a PhD degree in Finland and that in Canada boil down to pretty much a "research-driven" system versus a "school-driven" system. In Finland one is "research associate"; in Canada one is "PhD student". In Finland, one is paid a salary; in Canada one pays tuition (but may get a scholarship). In Finland the professor acts as the CEO of a company; in Canada the professor is the "supervisor" guiding the students. In Finland, courses are about the holistic experience; in Canada, courses are about marks and passing.

Being two completely different political entities, also the student body differs. In Finland, society is mainly mono-cultural with occasional streaks of xenophobia; in Canada, society is multi-cultural with the latest wave of immigrants hailing from South-East Asia. In Finland, PhD candidates usually continue straight from the Master's degree; in Canada many PhD students have an extensive record of previous employment in their native countries seeking a Canadian degree for access to the local labor market. In Finland the relationship with fellow PhD candidates is that of an extended student life suddenly turned into work life; in Canada it is that of a work life with the clock turned back often into a student life. In Finland one feels like a student suddenly empowered with a salary; in Canada one feels either like former employee reduced to the modest means of a student (immigrants) or just a student struggling on (natives).

I was now in the very fortunate situation to be able to exploit the advantages of both systems that somehow merged together in my two *alma mater*: The Finnish part at the Process Chemistry Centre of Åbo Akademi University had an uncharacteristically strong multicultural approach, while that of the Pulp and Paper Centre of University of Toronto was very research-driven with strong links to industry. The joint axis that brought both Centres together was the strong emphasis of their students or research associates to engage in extracurricular activities that hone the soft skills that are invaluable for employment afterwards. The clear goal of both institutions was to yield a crop that is easily employable in industry rather than nurturing their own academic needs for a future ivory tower.

Comparison of Finland – Germany

My frequent travels between Finland and Canada gave me the opportunity for frequent stopovers at home in Germany and keep in reasonably close contact with three fellow Master degree students who have opted to pursue a PhD at my first *alma mater*, the University of Dortmund.

As from their accounts I got the impression that in Germany one is employed either half time or full time to take over all kind of responsibilities that in my opinion ought to be in the professor's work description, like teaching students, writing fundraising applications, managing funds, administrating inter-university research projects and contributing to professors' books. The actual research seemed to be carried out in the spare time and compiling results into a thesis often appears years after the three-year contract ended and the former student has been employed for quite a while. In some cases, I observed that the thesis never materialized (with some other of my three close associates).

However, the obvious upside of taking over part of the professor's responsibilities is that one acquires part of the professor's organizational and leadership skills not just theoretically through courses and exercises but also hands-on by dealing with these issues on a daily basis. On the other side, the networking experience in Germany seemed to be rather on a national or pan-European level rather than on a truly international level as I was fortunate to experience in Finland and Canada.

However, since my account on a German PhD experience is strictly based on anecdotal evidence only, I must urge the reader to look for a more detailed analysis elsewhere in this book.

Academic Conclusion

What would be the academic outcome of my thesis? This is a question I have asked myself a couple of times since having acquired the degree. Certainly it was not the big bang of knowledge expansion that I may have fancied in my innocent beginnings of the PhD project, but it boiled down to rather some small steps in closing existing gaps of knowledge and laying a few bricks onto the wall of new ideas in my particular research topic.

Surely the recent good reputation from the PISA studies has helped to put Finland on the educational map and put the quality of the PhD degree earned beyond any doubt, but this would in my opinion be a too simplistic base for judgment.

Looking back, I must rather admit that I also contributed to what I would now call an inflation of scientific publications that one can observe since recent years. I am quite convinced that the results of my entire thesis could have been presented in two to three concise publications rather than the six publications accumulated in my thesis. True skill would have it to combine the entire thesis into one concise paper, and it may yet come so after the retirement of one of my professors.

The reason for this paper inflation is in my opinion quite easy to comprehend: Scientific standing and public funding of university research groups is directly linked to outputs of publication. As long as this system does not change the inflation is only bound to increase. Peer revision alone cannot really act as a damper to this inflation as one peer continues to be the other's peer…

Personal Conclusion

Opting from the beginning of my studies to not pursue any academic career, would I think that the time of my PhD studies was professionally lost and all that remains from the four years in Finland and Canada is the memory of experiencing merely the best years of my life? Absolutely not!

While I am no more writing papers, neither conducting any research, nor making use of the expansive network that I built up during my PhD experience, I certainly do make use of the hopefully in sufficient quantities acquired skills of organizing my thoughts and compiling complex matters into concise reports and clearly understandable presentations. In an industrial environment, this feat is called "executive summary" and required rather frequently. In addition, the practice of breaking down complex topics (like a PhD thesis or say, a 50 M€ project) into smaller and more understandable sub-projects is the basis of my daily work. Another now indispensable quality acquired during my PhD program is the experience in dealing with intercultural matters particularly involving South East Asian and American cooperation partners.

Personally, the PhD experience was particularly enriching my social life. As mentioned already a couple of times before, these years were amongst the very best of my life, and elaborating on these good times may fill yet an entire book. However, these good times are not just a memory from the past on which I may reflect on any given moment in the future, but they are also a part of daily life since I am maintaining a quite close relationship to former comrades in arms both from academic and non-academic backgrounds. While the friendships made in Finland are owing to the ERASMUS program rather of a pan-European nature stretching from Portugal to Russia, those made in Canada are more widely international.

An interesting question that may be worth elaborating is whether a PhD degree is actually worth the efforts from a financial point of view. Having obtained the PhD in a scientific rather than in a humanities field, I have realistic numbers available and can do this calculation quite easily. I must honestly admit it is the first time ever I follow through this calculation, believe it or not.

Let's just assume for simplicity's sake a starting salary (all numbers gross) of 45 k€ annually for a non-PhD engineer and of 60 k€ for a PhD engineer; a starting age of 25 years for the non-PhD engineer and of 30 years for a PhD engineer; a starting salary of 30 k€ for the PhD engineer while earning the degree in five years; a retirement age of 67 years and an annual salary increase of 3% in both cases. The total sum earned until retirement turns out as follows: 3.85 M€ for the non-PhD engineer and of 4.31 M€ for the PhD engineer. A whopping difference over working lifetime (not covering pensions) of half a million euros! The benefit lines of the non-PhD and PhD engineer cross at the age of just 38 years.

So actually it seems to be clearly paying off financially to pursue a PhD in engineering. But should that be the sole reason for pursuing a PhD? In my opinion, no. Would you expect to ascend to a higher position holding a PhD degree? Possibly yes, but not necessarily so. There are enough examples to the contrary, including board members of the multinational company that I am currently employed with. It's not like that a PhD degree stipulates you as a smarter person, but it's just more likely that a higher percentage of smart people may decide to pursue a PhD than otherwise.

Given the summary of the entire narrative above, would I do it again? The answer is: absolutely yes. But I'd be motivated rather by the prospect of living the best four years of my life again rather than the prospect of earning more money in the future.

Notes on Contributors

Agnieszka Bitner

2002, MA, Academy of Music, Katowice, Poland (Faculty of Drama and Opera). 2007, MA, Åbo; Akademi University (Germanic Philology, Polish Philology). 2010, Licentiate of Philosophy (FL), Åbo; Akademi University (Germanic Philology). 2008–2010 fee-paid teacher, German Department, Åbo; Akademi University. 2012, PhD, Mainz University (Slavic Philology/Polish Philology). Main research interests: Richard Wagner and his music drama, Polish translations of Wagner's dramas, translation science. E-mail: abitner@daad-alumni.de

Arzu Çöltekin

Bsc, Yildiz Technical University, 1995 (Geodesy and Photogrammetry - IAESTE Fellow, TU Delft, Netherlands, 1994). MSc, Yildiz Technical University, 1997 (Photogrammetry/GIS - CIMO Fellow, Helsinki University of Technology, 1997). PhD, Helsinki University of Technology, 2006 (Photogrammetry and Remote Sensing). Post-doc, Media Lab, University of Art and Design Helsinki (2006–2007). Senior Researcher and Lecturer, Group Leader at the Department of Geography, University of Zurich, Switzerland. Main research interests: geographic visualization, virtual reality, user experience, eye tracking. E-mail: arzu.coltekin@geo.uzh.ch. Homepage: http://www.geo.uzh.ch/~arzu/. Twitter: @acolt.

Jukka M. Krisp

Professor (W2) Angewandte Geoinformatik (Applied Geoinformatics) Universität Augsburg; 2013 Habilitation (Facultas Docendi), Technische Universität München (TUM); 2008–2013 Technische Universität München (TUM), Faculty of Civil Engineering and Geodesy, Department of Cartography; 2006–2008 Helsinki University of Technology (TKK) - Aalto-University, Department of Cartography & Geoinformatics; 2006 Doctor of Science in Technology (TkT), Helsinki University of Technology (TKK) - Aalto-University, Finland; 2003 Licentiate of Science in Technology (TkL), Helsinki University of Technology (TKK) - Aalto-University, Finland; 2001–2006 Helsinki University of Technology (TKK) - Aalto-University, Researcher, Department of Cartography & Geoinformatics;

2000 Diplom Geograph (Dipl.Geogr.); 1994–2000 Studies of Geography, Ruhr-Universität Bochum (RUB) & University of Turku, Finland; current research interests include Geovisualization, Location Based Services (LBS), Geographic Information Systems (GIS) and applications in civil protection & environmental modeling. E-mail: jukka.krisp@geo.uni-augsburg.de

Andreas McKeough

MA, University of Helsinki, 2008 (Folklore Studies). Doctoral candidate and researcher since 2009: University of Helsinki, University of Turku, University of Tartu, the Finnish Literature Society. Funding: the Research Foundation of the University of Helsinki, the Research School of Cultural Interpretations, Academy of Finland. Main research interests: narratives, narrative psychology, collective memory and cognitive cultural theory. Trainee in the Finnish Labour Archives, 2008. E-mail: andreas.mckeough@mappi.helsinki.fi

Piret Paal

MA, University of Tartu, 2004 (Estonian and Comparative Folklore). PhD, University of Helsinki, 2011 (Folkloristics). Since 2010 research fellow at the Ludwig-Maximilians-Universität München, Campus Großhadern, Department of Palliative Medicine. Main research interests: spirituality in healthcare, comprehensive healthcare models, spiritual care competencies and training for healthcare professionals. E-mail: Piret.Paal@med.uni-muenchen.de

Tarmo Pikner

MSc, University of Turku, 2000 (Human Geography). PhD, University of Oulu, 2008 (Human Geography). Advisor of regional planning at the Estonian Ministry of the Interior (2000–2002). Research fellow at the Ruhr-University Bochum (in 2003). Researcher at the Department of Geography at the University of Oulu (2004–2007); research fellow and lecturer at the Centre for Landscape and Culture, Estonian Institute of Humanities, Tallinn University (2008-present). Published in several peer-reviewed journals and in edited books. Main research interests: urban cultures, alternative mappings within landscape change, affects of late-modernity, vernacular knowledge ecologies. E-mail: tarmo.pikner@tlu.ee

Rangsima Sunila

D.Sc., Helsinki University of Technology, 2009 (Geoinformatics). MTM, University of New South Wales, 2000 (Technology Management). B.Sc., Mahidol University, 1997 (Mathematics). International Business Acumen (IBA), Helsinki Polytechnic 2003. Main research interests: Geostatistics, Fuzzy logic, Uncertainty in Geographical Information System. Visiting lecturer at Department of Real Estate, Planning and Geoinformatics, Aalto University. Co-founder and Business developer, Future Education Center. E-mail: rangsima.sunila@gmail.com

Michael Szurawitzki

MA, University of Turku, 2002 (English Philology). PhD, Åbo Akademi University, 2005 (Germanic Philology). Fulbright Fellow, University of California at Irvine, 2007. Adjunct Professor of Germanic Linguistics and Literature, Åbo Akademi University, 2009. Habilitation, Regensburg University, 2011 (Germanic Linguistics). Acting Professor of Germanic Linguistics at the University of Eastern Finland (2010), Siegen (2011), Duisburg-Essen (2011/2012), Ludwig-Maximilians-Universität München (2012/2013). Visiting professor, Tongji University, Shanghai (spring 2014). Main research interests: academic discourse, contrastive linguistics, text linguistics. E-mail: michael.szurawitzki@lmu.de. Web: www.szurawitzki.de. Ca. 100 academic publications, including four monographs and seven edited volumes.

Mischa Theis

1996–2001 Dortmund University, Diplom-Ingenieur (engineer), Chemical Technology. 2000–2001 Exchange Student, University of Toronto. 2002–2006 Åbo Akademi University, Turku, Finland: Process Chemnistry Centre; Doctor of Technology: Dissertation *Interaction of Biomass Fly Ashes with Different Fouling Tendencies.* 2006–2011 Bayer Technology Services, Leverkusen. Environmental Technologies and Waste Gas Incineration. Since 2011: Bayer CropScience AG, Monheim. Process Technology Active Ingredients APAC. E-mail: mischa.theis@bayer.com

Arbeit, Bildung & Gesellschaft
Labour, Education & Society

Herausgegeben von Prof. Dr. György Széll, Prof. Dr. Heinz Sünker,
Dr. Anne Inga Hilsen und Dr. Francesco Garibaldo

Bd. 1 György Széll (ed.): Corporate Social Responsibility in the EU & Japan. 2006.

Bd. 2 Katja Maar: Zum Nutzen und Nichtnutzen der Sozialen Arbeit am exemplarischen Feld der Wohnungslosenhilfe. Eine empirische Studie. 2006.

Bd. 3 Daniela De Ridder: Vom urbanen Sozialraum zur kommunikativen Stadtgesellschaft. 2007.

Bd. 4 Heinz Sünker / Ingrid Miethe (Hrsg.): Bildungspolitik und Bildungsforschung: Herausforderungen und Perspektiven für Gesellschaft und Gewerkschaften in Deutschland. 2007.

Bd. 5 Anja Bastigkeit: Bildungsbiographie und elementarpädagogische Bildungsarbeit. 2007.

Bd. 6 Antônio Inácio Andrioli: Biosoja versus Gensoja. Eine Studie über Technik und Familienlandwirtschaft im nordwestlichen Grenzgebiet des Bundeslandes Rio Grande do Sul (Brasilien). 2007.

Bd. 7 Russell Farnen / Daniel German / Henk Dekker / Christ'l De Landtsheer / Heinz Suenker (eds.): Political Culture, Socialization, Democracy, and Education. Interdisciplinary and Cross-National Perspectives for a New Century. 2008.

Bd. 8 Francesco Garibaldo / Volker Telljohann (eds.): New Forms of Work Organisation and Industrial Relations in Southern Europe. 2007.

Bd. 9 Anne Marie Berg / Olav Eikeland (eds.): Action Research and Organisation Theory. 2008.

Bd. 10 György Széll / Carl-Heinrich Bösling / Ute Széll (eds.): Education, Labour & Science. Perspectives for the 21st Century. 2008.

Bd. 11 Francesco Garibaldo / Philippe Morvannou / Jochen Tholen (eds.): Is China a Risk or an Opportunity for Europe? An Assessment of the Automobile, Steel and Shipbuilding Sectors. 2008.

Bd. 12 Yunus Dauda: Managing Technology Innovation. The Human Resource Management Perspective. 2009.

Bd. 13 Jarmo Lehtonen / Satu Kalliola (eds.): Dialogue in Working Life Research and Development in Finland. 2009.

Bd. 14 György Széll / Werner Kamppeter / Woosik Moon (eds.): European Social Integration – A Model for East Asia? 2009.

Bd. 15 Benedicte Brøgger / Olav Eikeland (eds.): Turning to Practice with Action Research. 2009.

Bd. 16 Till Johannes Hoffmann: Verschwendung. Philosophie, Soziologie und Ökonomie des Überflusses. 2009.

Bd. 17 Denis Harrisson / György Széll / Reynald Bourque (eds.): Social Innovation, the Social Economy and World Economic Development. 2009.

Bd. 18 Werner Weltgen: Total Quality Management als Strukturierungsaufgabe für nachhaltigen Unternehmenswandel. 2009.

Bd. 19 György Széll / Ute Széll (eds.): Quality of Life and Working Life in Comparison. 2009.

Bd. 20 Francesco Garibaldo / Volker Telljohann (eds.): The Ambivalent Character of Participation. New Tendencies in Worker Participation in Europe. 2010.

Bd. 21 Richard Ennals / Robert H. Salomon (eds.): Older Workers in a Sustainable Societey. 2011.

Bd. 22   Christoph Sänger: Anna Siemsen – Bildung und Literatur. 2011.
Bd. 23   Nam-Kook Kim: Deliberative Multiculturalism in Britain. A Response to Devolution, European Integration, and Multicultural Challenges. 2011.
Bd. 24   Mirella Baglioni / Bernd Brandl (eds.): Changing Labour Relations. Between Path Dependency and Global Trends. 2011.
Bd. 25   Rüdiger Kühr: Japan`s Transnational Environmental Policies. The Case of Environmental Technology Transfer to Newly Industrializing Countries. 2011.
Bd. 26   Francesco Garibaldo / Dinghong Yi (eds.): Labour and Sustainable Development. North-South Perspectives. 2012.
Bd. 27   Francesco Garibaldo / Mirella Baglioni / Catherine Casey / Volker Telljohann (eds.): Workers, Citizens, Governance. Socio-Cultural Innovation at Work. 2012.
Bd. 28   Simone Selva: Supra-National Integration and Domestic Economic Growth. The United States and Italy in the Western Bloc Rearmament Programs 1945-1955. Translation by Filippo del Lucchese, revision by Simone Selva. 2012.
Band 29 György Széll / Roland Czada (Hrsg.): Fukushima. Die Katastrophe und ihre Folgen. 2013.
Band 30 Siqi Luo: Collective Bargaining and Changing Industrial Relations in China. Lessons from the U. S. and Germany. 2013.
Band 31 Litsa Nicolaou-Smokoviti / Heinz Sünker / Julia Rozanova / Victoria Pekka Economou (eds.): Citizenship and Social Development. Citizen Participation and Community Involvement in Social Welfare and Social Policy. 2013.
Band 32 Christ'l De Landtsheer / Russell F. Farnen / Daniel B. German / Henk Dekker / Heinz Sünker / Yingfa Song / Hongna Miao (eds.): E-Political Socialization, the Press and Politics. The Media and Government in the USA, Europe and China. 2014.
Band 33 Jukka M. Krisp / Michael Szurawitzki (eds.): Doctoral Experiences in Finland. 2014.

www.peterlang.com

www.ingramcontent.com/pod-product-compliance
Ingram Content Group UK Ltd.
Pitfield, Milton Keynes, MK11 3LW, UK
UKHW021830140426
5217IPUK00021B/1366